The Secret of
Challah

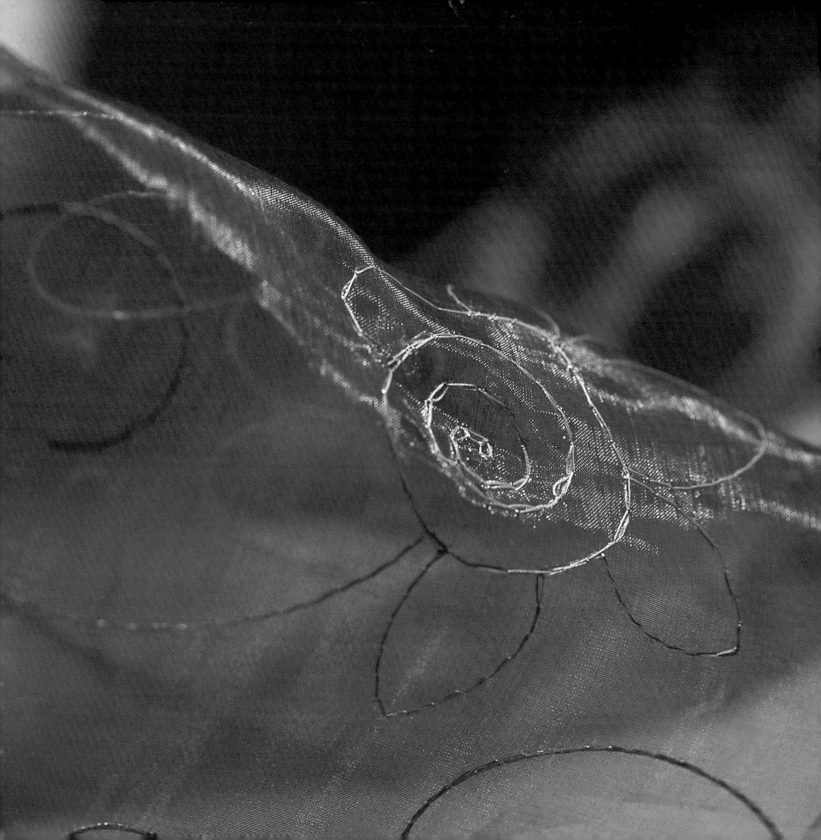

The Secret of
Challah

Shira Wiener
&
Ayelet Yifrach

Photographs by Tamar Kinarty

לקראת חלה

שירה וינר ואילת יפרח

Photographs: Tamar Kinarty (Pais)

Illustrations: Anat Berenson

Editorial Production: Shoshanna Makover

Design by Reshit Studios

Published by

RESHIT PUBLICATIONS

29 Hashalom St. Rosh Pinna, Israel 12000

Tel: 972-4-693-6770

www.challah-book.com

ISBN 978-965-90779-2-2

Printed in Israel by Keter Press, Jerusalem

To our daughters, with all our love

20 Shevat 5765   בס"ד

Haskamah

I have shown manuscript of the important work "Likrat Challah" for Jewish women, which contains a significant chapter on the laws of separating challah. The chapter presents the basic laws of the procedure of separating challah in a clear language accessible to all, for both women and girls.

It is important to stress, however, that while the basic halachah is that we do not "reject" a person who makes the blessing upon separating challah according to Rav Chaim Naeh's measurements, especially since, according to the *Be'ur Halachah* (271), we can rely on the smaller measurements (i.e., that of Rav Naeh) when it comes to *mitzvot derabbanan*, nevertheless, it is the opinion of HaGaon Rav Asher Weiss that ideally and whenever possible it is proper to be meticulous and make the blessing on the amount of dough specified by the Chazon Ish.

I bless the noteworthy authors that as a result of this important work, blessing should rest upon the homes of all Jewish women, as the *pasuk* says, "You shall give the first yield of your dough to the kohen to make a blessing rest upon your home" (*Yechezkel* 44:30).

Rabbi Chaim Vidal
Member of the Beit Din Tzedek

MORDECHAI ELIAHU
FORMER CHIEF RABBI OF ISRAEL & RICHON LEZION

מרדכי אליהו
הראשון לציון והרב הראשי לישראל לשעבר

13 Shevat 5765

Haskamah

When G-d created man, He took earth from the soil of all the world, added water to it, kneaded it like dough, and blew into it the breath of life. Our Sages tell us that at that moment, the whole world was like a large amount of dough, and Adam – the first man – was separated from it like "the challah of the world."

Challah is the portion of dough given to G-d – that is, to the *kohen*. It is the part dedicated for Holiness. Challah binds together the bread, its consumption and the physical world to be in oneness with Holiness. Without *challah* – the separated portion, bread is forbidden, and yet when the mitzvah of separation is fulfilled, the bread is blessed and permitted to be eaten. Herein lies man's purpose in the world: In his deeds he gives it meaning, direction, connection to holiness, and the right to be.

Our Sages laid great importance on baking challah for Shabbat (see *Shulchan Aruch, Orach Chaim 242, Rema*). When performed by a woman, they considered it to have even greater value, being *"hiddur mitzvah"* (beautifying the commandment). The mitzvah is then more beloved, since "Doing a mitzvah by oneself is greater than that which is done by his envoy."

The Kabbalistic Sages wrote in the name of the Ari *(Sha'ar HaKavanot)* that one gains merit for baking twelve loaves of challah for the meals of Shabbat, as they contain a trace of holiness and a taste of the twelve loaves of showbread that were in the *Beit HaMikdash*. They also wrote that even a woman who buys challah from the bakery all year round should try, at least once a year, to bake her own challah and fulfill the mitzvah of separating the challah from the dough with a blessing.

The Ben Ish Hai writes in his halachic work that the appropriate time to do this is during the Ten Days of Repentance, when we are in the process of rectifying the damage caused by us and previous generations, and that done by Adam and Chavah in the Garden of Eden, whose sin we continuously seek to repair.

I bless the authors for their efforts in writing this special book, which seeks to inspire others to beautify the precious mitzvah of baking challah for Shabbat and fulfill the exalted mitzvah – *Hafrashat Challah* – separating challah, which accompanies it.

With blessings,

Rabbi Mordechai Eliahu
Rishon Letzion and former Chief Rabbi of Israel

Preface

I always loved to bake. I remember as if it were today, the first cookies I baked as a young girl – the sensation of excitement being in the kitchen, the wonder of magic in turning the mixture of ingredients into tasty crispy cookies; but most of all – I remember the enjoyment of eating and sharing the cookies with my family.

As I grew up, I started dreaming about *challahs*. Compared to cookies, this felt like "the Real Thing." Ever since I was a girl I had a special fondness for anything that had the aroma of *Yidishkeit*. Challahs were such. In the baking of challahs there's a feeling of baking something of real value – a sensation that is accompanied by the taste of the sweetness in the holiness of Shabbat.

While kneading the dough, I would imagine myself as an experienced housewife that knows her chores well. Kneading the dough with rhythm and confidence was something that I envisioned our mothers doing through the ages.

As a beginner in the art of baking, dealing with the yeast was fascinating and intriguing. An issue full of question marks: What is the secret of the yeast bubbling in the bowl? What do you do when the dough sticks to your hands and to anything else in hand? (I came to learn that the skilled movements of kneading are not exactly in our born nature...) What does it mean when the recipe book says "Its size will be doubled"? Mistrusting, I would peep under the towel every few minutes to check if the dough had already swollen-up and try to assess if it had already doubled its size.

I didn't even think about *hafrashat challah*. That seemed an operation too complicated for me to tackle. And as in those days back home, we didn't yet take to the baking of challahs, I was afraid

I wouldn't know exactly how to fulfill the mitzvah of separating the challah. What was the right quantity needed for *hafrashat challah*? And what should I do afterwards with the piece I've separated? This was the reason I always baked in small quantities, so that I need not cope with all these questions.

During my studies in university, one of my writing assignments was on *hafrashat challah*. For the first time, I sat down to read into the material and study it in depth. Only then, did I learn about the contents of the mitzvah and only then did I realize how easy it is to earn it. Moreover, I learnt of the many *"segulot"* – virtues that are concealed within the mitzvah of *hafrashat challah*.

That very day, the idea of writing this book came to my mind (in Hebrew we say came to my heart, which is truer in my case) – to write for Jewish women who dreamt to bake challahs; A book that would help them do it with with ease and *"nachat ruach"*.

I would like to take this opportunity to thank my sister, my whole-hearted devoted partner – Ayelet, for assisting me to make my dream come true. It is she, that has given the book form and design and it is she, who is responsible for its special charm. Together, we made an effort to bring you – the challah baker, all the relevant information needed in the clearest, easiest and most coherent way. We included also sayings from the fountains of the Torah – the soul and depth of the mitzvah of *hafrashat challah*.

I hope this book will be an answer to all your questions concerning the art of baking challahs and that you will find the task itself enjoyable.

May G-d's blessing dwell in your homes and prevail in all your deeds.

Shira

CONTENTS

RECIPES

THE ART OF BRAIDING

THE
BLESSING
IN THE
DOUGH

Challah Baking:
A Divine Experience

וַיְדַבֵּר ה' אֶל־מֹשֶׁה לֵּאמֹר: דַּבֵּר אֶל־בְּנֵי יִשְׂרָאֵל וְאָמַרְתָּ אֲלֵהֶם בְּבֹאֲכֶם
אֶל הָאָרֶץ אֲשֶׁר אֲנִי מֵבִיא אֶתְכֶם שָׁמָּה: וְהָיָה בַּאֲכָלְכֶם מִלֶּחֶם הָאָרֶץ
תָּרִימוּ תְרוּמָה לַה': רֵאשִׁית עֲרִסֹתֵכֶם חַלָּה תָּרִימוּ תְרוּמָה כִּתְרוּמַת
גֹּרֶן כֵּן תָּרִימוּ אֹתָהּ: מֵרֵאשִׁית עֲרִסֹתֵיכֶם תִּתְּנוּ לַה' תְּרוּמָה לְדֹרֹתֵיכֶם:

*"G-d spoke to Moshe, saying: 'Speak to the children of Israel,
and say to them: When you come to the land to which I bring
you, it shall be that when you will eat of the bread of the land,
you shall offer up a gift to the L-rd. From the first portion of
your dough you shall set aside a loaf as a portion, like the
portion from the threshing floor, so shall you set it aside. From
the first portion of your dough you shall give to the L-rd an
offering throughout your generations.'"* (Numbers 15:17-21)

The Jewish people first became obligated to perform the mitzvah of
separating challah *(hafrashat challah)* when they entered the Land
of Israel. The mitzvah requires a person to set aside a portion of the
dough that is to be baked into bread. This portion of dough is given to
the *kohanim* (priests who served in the Temple), allowing them to live
honorably and to fullfil their holy tasks in comfort. Since bread is man's
primary source of sustenance, separating challah is a commandment
that is applicable at all times, and it brings blessing into our daily lives.

When the majority of Jews are living in the Land of Israel, *hafrashat
challah* is a Torah obligation. The Torah does not specify exactly how
much dough must be separated, but our Sages have determined that
someone who bakes bread at home must separate 1/24 of the dough,
and a commercial baker is obligated to separate 1/48 of his dough.

When the majority of Jews are not living in the Land of Israel, *hafrashat challah* is a *mitzvah derabbanan*, a precept of rabbinic rather than Torah origin. The Sages established that the separated piece of dough be the size of a *kazayit* (literally, "the size of an olive"), practically speaking, 28 grams (about an ounce), or the size of a ping-pong ball. *Hafrashat challah* is observed in Eretz Israel and everywhere outside it, so that the mitzvah of *challah* will not be forgotten.

The piece of dough that is separated is called "challah." The word for the bread we eat on Shabbat is taken from this term. The separated piece of dough may be eaten only by *kohanim* who are ritually pure. Today, as long as the Temple is not rebuilt, everyone is considered impure, including the *kohanim*, and our challah too is impure. We may not give it to a kohen, nor may we eat it or derive benefit from it. We must therefore ensure that the separated challah will be rendered inedible. It should be burned or disposed of respectfully, since it contains an element of holiness.

Every moment of every day, we eagerly await the arrival of Mashiach (The True Redeemer) and the return of all the Jewish people to the Land of Israel, and the rebuilding of the Holy Temple. We will then, once again, be able to perform the mitzvah of *hafrashat challah* fully, and in sanctity.

Divine Providence in the Kitchen

What a wonderful aroma fills the house when our home baked bread comes out of the oven, all the effort we put into it feels worthwhile. We have sifted the flour, added ingredients according to the recipe and a little according to our intuitions, kneaded the dough, waited for it to rise, and finally have placed the braided dough into the oven.

When we hear the praise for the beautiful challahs we have made, feelings of pride and satisfaction may steal their way into our hearts. It is natural to attribute this success to the recipe that we received from a neighbor, or to a special spice or ingredient that we added, or to the many years of experience we have with baking.

Amid the mixing bowls and sifted flour, the egg for glazing and sprinkling of sesame seeds to add just the right touch, we should remember the source of our success and perform the mitzvah of *hafrashat challah*.

The Torah commands us to separate a portion of the dough we have put so much effort into making, and to dedicate it to the Holy One Blessed be He. We must remember that it is more than just our talents and skills that have produced these challahs. G-d's blessing and Divine Providence are present in everything we do, as well as in the challahs that we make.

The wheat farmer, too, is commanded to separate a portion of his crop. Like the homemaker with her bread, the farmer invests much energy and effort in his field. He plows, plants, and is gratified when he sees his hard labor bear fruit. The farmer, though, is also constantly aware of his dependence on G-d's benevolent kindness for the success of his crop. He humbly faces the forces of nature, and prays to G-d for the blessing of rain. Finally, when the crops grow and ripen, the farmer takes the fruits of his labor and tithes a portion of it *(terumah* and *ma'aser)*.

The mitzvah of *hafrashat challah* reminds us that Divine Providence goes beyond G-d's dominance over the forces of nature. Divine Providence continues to guide us as we knead dough in the kitchen, as it does in everything we do. That is why challah is separated from the dough, which we ourselves have prepared, and not from the flour in its raw form. This is our way of expressing the recognition that the Creator oversees every detail of our lives, and it is He who blesses the fruits of our labors.

A Blessing in the Home

Hafrashat challah is one of the special mitzvahs entrusted to the Jewish woman. A man separates challah only when there is no woman in the home, or when the woman grants him permission to perform the mitzvah.

The first time that the mitzvah of *hafrashat challah* is referred to in the Torah is in connection with our Mothers Sarah and Rivkah. When the angels came to visit Avraham, he personally went to prepare a meal in their honor, as it is written: "Avraham ran to the cattle, took a calf, tender and good... He took cream and milk and the calf that he had prepared..." (Genesis 18:7-8). He did all this with tremendous love for the mitzvah of welcoming guests. The making of bread, however, he left to his wife, because that mitzvah belonged to her: "Avraham rushed to Sarah's tent, and he said, 'Quikly, get three se'ah of sifted flour, knead them and make loaves!' " (Genesis 18:6).

When Yitzhak brought Rivkah to the tent of his mother, Sarah, the three miracles that had been present during her lifetime, returned:

> *"'Yitzhak brought her into the tent of Sarah, his mother' – She became like Sarah his mother, for as long as Sarah lived, the candle light burned from one Shabbat to the next, there was blessing in the dough, and a cloud hovered over her tent. When she died, the miracles ceased, but when Rivkah came, they returned."*
>
> (Genesis 24:67 and *Rashi* there)

The reappearance of these three signs proved to Yitzhak that Rivkah was fitting to continue the path of his mother, Sarah.

The three miracles in Sarah's tent allude to the three mitzvahs unique to women. Through the fulfillment of these mitzvahs a woman merits to establish her home on the basis of a firm foundation, and to bring G-d's blessing into it. The candle signifies the lighting of the Shabbat candles and the unique quality women are blessed with for bringing light, warmth and spiritual content into the home. The cloud atop the tent symbolizes the Divine presence that rests on a home where the laws of family purity are observed. The blessing in the dough alludes to the mitzvah of *hafrashat challah*, as it says: "You shall give the first yield of your dough to the kohen to make a blessing rest upon your home" (Ezekiel 44:30).

The Woman's Central Role

The mitzvah of *hafrashat challah* has the unique ability to bring G-d's blessing into the Jewish home. The baking of bread is symbolic of the woman's central role as a homemaker. When she performs the mitzvah of *hafrashat challah*, she shows her recognition and awareness of G-d's intervention in all of her daily activities and actions.

Sometimes the never-ending occupation with housework can bring about a sense of emptiness and meaninglessness. What personal or spiritual growth is there in washing dishes, cleaning the floor, or preparing supper? We may think: have my efforts added anything significant or meaningful to the world?

An answer can be found in the commandments related to keeping kosher (observing Jewish dietary laws). These mitzvahs provide us with the opportunity to conduct our homes in accordance with the Divine will and to put a mark of holiness on the food we prepare for our families. When a woman checks rice for insects, sifts flour, or is very careful regarding the separation of meat and milk, she is fulfilling G-d's will that we eat kosher foods. Reflecting on that aspect may provide us with renewed energies and meaning to the preparation of food.

It is for a good reason that in Hebrew the woman of the house is referred to as the *akeret habayit* – "the foundation of the home." The various labors that she performs, like her spiritual work, are carried out within the walls of her home. A woman is compared to a kohen working in the Holy Temple. It may seem that the kohen is doing work of a very material nature, such as slaughtering animals, sprinkling blood, and other physical tasks in the Temple, however, all of his actions are carried out with the intention of fulfilling the will of the Holy One Blessed be He. Just as G-d chose to have His presence dwell in the Holy Temple, which was merely a structure of wood and stone made by man, so too, His presence dwells in every Jewish home. The woman's role in the home empowers her with the ability to make her home into a vessel for receiving and emanating G-d's blessing.

Here, in the sanctuary of her home, the woman is graced with the special capacity to converse with her Creator, and the chance to add her personal touch of love and faith to the bread, the sustenance, that she serves to her family.

"The Challah of the World"

Man's Mission

The last and the most dear of G-d's creation was man. All of the other creations – heaven and earth, plants and trees, animals and birds – were created so that man would be able to fulfill the Divine mission for which he was created: To reveal the existence of G-d in the world.

A superficial view of the world can be deceiving. Every day the sun rises in the east and sets in the west. A tiny seedling becomes a blossoming tree. Minuscule cells work together in perfect coordination. All the forces of nature seemingly operate independently and on their own in perfect harmony. This natural cause-and-effect camouflages the true cause: The Creator of the world, He who governs the world and endows it with life.

Into this world of concealment man was sent. His mission is to find the Godliness that exists within our physical, materialistic world. In doing so, we link spiritual with the material aspect of the world, enabling the Divine presence to dwell on earth, and bring the ultimate redemption.

This mission seems impossible to fulfill. How can we accomplish it?

The Midrash refers to Adam as the "challah of the world" because of the unique manner in which he was created. G-d gathered dust from all the ends of the earth and mixed it with water, creating a clay, similar to the way one creates a dough. With this mixture G-d created man.

Thus, man was created from dust, the lowliest element in creation. But then G-d breathed into man a soul, a part of Himself. Man, therefore, contains two opposite elements: a physical body and a Divine soul. This duality enables him to perceive in spite of concealment and to effect unity in places of separateness, bringing the entire world closer to its goal: harmony between the spiritual and the material, between heaven and earth, between the world and its Creator.

Unlike man, who was created from dust, woman was created from a higher level of raw material: Adam's rib. When describing the creation of Chavah, the first woman, the Torah uses the word *vayyiven*, "to build." This alludes to the power with which woman was blessed, the power to build and influence, which enables her to fulfill her task of building a home and serving as a fitting helper and strong foundation to her husband.

Descending in order to Ascend

Our Sages say: "A person does not sin unless a spirit of foolishness enters him" *(Sotah 3a)*. In a moment of foolishness, Chavah incited Adam to partake from the Tree of Knowledge. After this sin, the world's spiritual level descended. The manifestation of the Divine presence receded, darkness in the world increased and evil mingled with good. The phenomena of death and cessation became an integral part of the creation.

Before Adam and Chavah sinned, evil resided outside man; it was a separate entity. The sin of the Tree of Knowledge caused evil to become an intrinsic part of reality. The outcome of this was a new mission for man: to distinguish and separate the good from the evil, to expose the kernel of truth hidden inside everything in this world, and to struggle against the elements of evil that could now be found in himself. This is a complex and enduring mission, which, throughout the ages, man has been striving to accomplish and fulfill.

Every moment of our lives, everything in creation, every blade of grass, is governed by Divine Providence. Adam and Chavah's sin was not just an accidental happening. Kabbalah teaches us that within every evil thing there is a kernel of Divine truth waiting to be revealed. What appears to be a descent, or even a terrible fall, may actually be a step toward the discovery of a hidden good. The purpose of sin is the ascent that can follow when a rectification of the sin *(tikkun)* is made. A proper *tikkun* does more than just mend broken parts together; it brings with it a degree of perfection that did not exist previously.

The fall of Adam and Chavah was part of G-d's plan. Since the fall was so great, we know that the *tikkun* it will effect will bring about an ascent that is even greater. The ongoing *tikkun* of Adam and Chavah's sin is what will eventually bring the ultimate redemption.

Through the woman the incident of the Tree of Knowledge evolved as it did, and it is the woman who is endowed with the special powers to effect a *tikkun*. In order that she be able to realize the potential of these powers, G-d gave her three unique mitzvahs which will help her bring about the *tikkun*: family purity, separating challah, and the lighting of shabbat candles.

> *"Why was woman given the mitzvah of family purity? Because she 'spilled the blood' of Adam – because of this she was given the mitzvah of family purity. Why was she given the mitzvah of challah? Because she caused Adam to sin and he was considered the 'challah of the world' – because of this she was given the mitzvah of challah. Why was she given the mitzvah of lighting the Shabbat candles? He said to them: Because she brought about the death of Adam, whose soul is compared to a candle – because of this she was given the mitzvah of lighting Shabbat candles."*
>
> (Midrash, *Bereshit Rabbah* 17:13)

Man's role in this world is divided into three categories, based on the verse: "Turn away from evil and do good, seek peace and pursue it" (Psalms 34:15). The three mitzvahs unique to women correspond to these three categories: By observing the laws of family purity, keeping our distance from impurity, we observe the exhortation to "turn away from evil." By separating challah, we add sanctity to food, thereby fulfilling "and do good." And the mitzvah of lighting Shabbat candles, which corresponds to "seek peace and pursue it," brings us closer to the rest and heavenly serenity of the eternal Sabbath (the seventh and last millennium - which is considered the "days of Mashiach").

These three mitzvahs are a great privilege – they give us the ability to establish our home on strong foundations and turn it into dwelling place for G-d's Divine presence. Since these mitzvahs effect a *tikkun* that touches upon the very root of existence, a woman merits, by fulfilling and observing them, to elevate the entire world to a level of completeness more exalted than the one that existed at the time of creation.

Preparing Bread,
Building the Soul

Grinding

The process of making bread teaches us much about the process of inner spiritual development.

We start with a mound of wheat kernels. The kernels are hard and separate from one another; it is easy to distinguish one kernel from another. In order to produce flour, the kernels must be ground fine. It is only when the kernels lose their individual identities – when no remnant of their independent existence remains – that they become flour.

This is the first stage of inner development. The "kernel of grain" within us is the feeling of our separate, personal existence, which is deeply rooted in us. It is human nature to be focused on our personal needs and drives, our thoughts and emotions, our personal troubles and dreams. As long as we concentrate on ourselves, it is difficult to truly care about others. By solely looking to fulfill our own wants and needs, we are likely to fall prey to arrogance and apathy toward others.

"Spiritual grinding" is the effort we make to rise above our nature and our personal desires, which enables us to remove the "chaff" around our hearts and become more sensitive to others.

Kneading

The grinding is done. The flour is ready. To make the dough, we must now mix it with water.

The nature of water is to flow from a high place to a low place (tractate *Ta'anit* 7a), seemingly in a constant search. The moment it comes across a fissure or small crevice, it penetrates deep inside. From water we learn

23

to moderate our feelings of grandeur and search for ways to give to others, even when seemingly we are on different levels. Water's determination to reach the deepest places teaches us to let ourselves reach out to others, searching for every possible opening to the other person's heart.

There are many factors that contribute to a feeling of connection among people. At times, the workplace or classroom creates a solid social environment. Sometimes a powerful joint experience forges a special bond between people, and common ideals often bind individuals together. All of these relationships, however, hinge upon the presence or fulfillment of a certain factor – and are therefore limited. Were the factor to disappear, so would the unity.

By contrast, unity that stems from humility and a true desire to help others creates an unbreakable bond. As the water bonds the grains of flour into a unified mass of dough, so *tzedakah,* the giving of charity and helping others, creates an enduring bond between people. Such is the quality of *tzedakah,* which is equated to all the other mitzvahs.

Baking

The act of kneading has created a new entity. We no longer have two components, flour and water, but one mass of dough. Now comes the next stage of transformation: The dough is placed in the oven to be baked. When it comes out of the oven, it is no longer called "dough," but "bread," as it says in Psalms 104:15: "And bread that sustains man's heart."

Bread gives life and nourishment to man, making it possible for the soul to dwell in the human body, and for man to utilize the gifts that G-d bestowed upon him, and fulfill his mission in this world.

The material in this chapter is based on various discourses and writings of the Lubavitcher Rebbe.

The Mitzvah of Hafrashat Challah

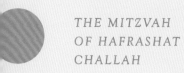
When is Challah Separated?

In order to determine whether our dough requires separating challah, and whether we should separate challah with a blessing or without a blessing, we must consider the type and the amount of flour used and the liquid contents of the dough.

Type of Flour

The obligation to separate challah applies to dough made with flour produced from one of, or a combination of, the following five grains: **wheat, barley, rye, oat** and **spelt**.

Amount of Flour

The amount of flour used determines whether challah is separated with a blessing or without a blessing, or is not separated at all.

These are the amounts of flour required for separating challah (according to the opinion of Rabbi Chaim Naeh; see other opinions below):

● **Separate challah with a blessing:**
When using at least 1,666.6 grams (3 lbs. 10.8 oz.) of flour.

● **Separate challah without a blessing:**
When using flour weighing between 1,230 and 1,666.6 grams (between 2 lbs. 11.4 oz. and 3 lbs. 10.8 oz.).

● **Do not separate challah**:
When using less than 1,230 grams (2 lbs. 11.4 oz.) of flour.

Halachic Opinion	Separate Challah without a Blessing	Separate Challah with a Blessing
Rabbi Chaim Naeh	From 1,230 grams 2 lbs. 11.4 oz.	From 1,666.6 grams 3 lbs. 10.8 oz.
Chazon Ish	From 1,200 grams 2 lbs. 10.3 oz.	From 2,250 grams 4 lbs. 15.4 oz.
Rabbi Mordechai Eliyahu	From 1,666 grams 3 lbs. 10.8 oz.	From 2,486 grams 5 lbs. 7.7 oz.
Rabbi Ovadiah Yosef	From 1,615.3 grams 3 lbs. 9 oz.	From 1,666.5 grams 3 lbs. 10.8 oz.

All flour used when preparing the dough, such as flour used when rolling the dough, should be included in the calculations.

When Measuring Flour in Cups

It is preferable to measure the amount of flour in units of weight (grams, pounds, ounces) rather than in cups, because different types of flour have differences in moisture content, and the manner in which the flour is measured affects the measuring results. When flour is measured in cups, it is best to avoid the "gray areas" in the diagram below.

The Amount of Flour Required for Separating Challah - in Cups*

* The figures were calculated with a standard 8 oz. (230 cc) measuring cup containing sifted white flour. The figures were calculated based on the opinion of Rabbi Chaim Naeh.

Liquid Contents

In order that challah be separated from the dough, the majority of the dough's liquid content must be one of the following: water, wine, milk, bee honey, or olive oil.

There is a difference of halachic opinions as to whether the obligation to separate challah applies to dough whose liquid ingredients are only fruit juice or eggs. It is therefore preferable to add a bit of water, wine, milk, bee honey, or olive oil to the dough and separate challah without a blessing.

Different Types of Dough

The mitzvah of separating challah applies not only to challah or bread dough, but also to any dough that meets the requirements of flour and liquids as detailed above, such as the dough of cakes, cookies, and pizza.

If one prepares a dough or batter with the intention of cooking or frying it (such as doughnuts or blintzes), challah should be separated without a blessing. However, if one's intention is to bake even a small part of it, challah should be separated with a blessing.

Combining Doughs

When preparing more than one dough, and each dough does not have the required amount of flour needed to separate challah, the doughs may be combined, and challah can be separated.

If one is concerned that the different doughs should not get mixed together (such as bread dough and cake batter), they should not be joined.

To combine the doughs, lay them next to one another so that they touch, and separate challah with a blessing. If it is difficult to combine the doughs, one may leave them in their bowls and cover them with a cloth or some other covering so that they appear to be one mass of dough.

Separating Challah After Baking

Challah is usually separated from dough before it has been divided or shaped. In some cases, however, challah needs to be separated from the finished product, after the baking is done.

● When separating challah from cake batter, challah may be separated after the cake has been baked, since it is difficult to separate a portion of unbaked cake batter.

● If you have forgotten to separate challah from any type of dough before it was baked, you can separate challah after baking.

If you are separating challah from baked goods, cover them all with a cloth or place into one container. Then take a piece from one of the baked goods and say the blessing if required.

Remember not to partake of the baked goods until challah has been separated.

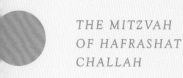

How to Separate Challah

1. *Place the dough in front of you, before it has been formed into any sort of shape.*

> If you are separating challah from a loose batter, or if you forgot to separate challah before baking, see above *"Separating Challah After Baking."*

2. *Some have the custom to give charity or wash hands (netilat yadayim) without a blessing before fulfilling the mitzvah.*

> This is a favorable time for personal requests and prayers (see prayers below).

3. *Recite the blessing.*

> It is the custom to stand while performing this mitzvah.

Ashkenazim:

בָּרוּךְ אַתָּה יְיָ אֱלֹהֵינוּ מֶלֶךְ הָעוֹלָם, אֲשֶׁר קִדְּשָׁנוּ בְּמִצְוֹתָיו, וְצִוָּנוּ לְהַפְרִישׁ חַלָּה [מִן הָעִסָּה].

Ba'ruch a'ta a'do'nai elo'hei'nu me'lech ha'o'lam, a'sher kid'sha'nu be'mitz'vo'tav ve'tzi'va'nu le'haf'rish challah [some add: min ha'i'sah].

Blessed are You, L-rd our G-d, King of the Universe, who has sanctified us with His commandments, and commanded us to separate challah [some add: from the dough].

Sephardim:

בָּרוּךְ אַתָּה יְיָ אֱלֹהֵינוּ מֶלֶךְ הָעוֹלָם, אֲשֶׁר קִדְּשָׁנוּ
בְּמִצְוֹתָיו, וְצִוָּנוּ לְהַפְרִישׁ חַלָּה תְרוּמָה.

*Ba'ruch a'ta a'do'nai elo'hei'nu me'lech
ha'o'lam, a'sher kid'sha'nu be'mitz'vo'tav
ve'tzi'va'nu le'haf'rish challah te'ru'mah.*

**Blessed are You, L-rd our G-d, King of the Universe,
who has sanctified us with His commandments, and
commanded us to separate challah terumah.**

4. *Remove a small piece from the dough, lift it, and say:*

הֲרֵי זוֹ חַלָּה   *Ha'rei zo challah*   **This is Challah**

The piece of dough can be of any size. The custom is to
separate a *kazayit* – 28 grams (approximately one ounce),
or the size of a ping-pong ball.

5. *Burn the separated dough or wrap it in two layers and
discard it.*

It is preferable to burn the piece of dough that has been
separated, but not in the oven. If the challah is burned on
the gas range, it should first be well wrapped in aluminum
foil so that the dough does not touch the grate. Another
option is to place the piece of dough inside a tin-can and
burn it on a lit gas range.

If burning the challah cannot easily be done, it may be
wrapped in two layers of a material such as aluminum foil
or plastic bags and discarded.

Prayers

The moment of separating challah is an especially propitious moment for praying for family and loved ones. You may, of course, offer a personal prayer in your own words, or you can say one of the following.

● Prayer to be recited before separating challah:

> יְהִי רָצוֹן מִלְפָנֶיךָ ה' אֱלֹהֵינוּ וֵאלֹהֵי אֲבוֹתֵינוּ שֶׁתְּבָרֵךְ
> עִסָּתֵנוּ כְּמוֹ שֶׁשָּׁלַחְתָּ בְּרָכָה בְּעִסּוֹת אִמּוֹתֵינוּ שָׂרָה, רִבְקָה,
> רָחֵל וְלֵאָה, וִיקֻיַּם בָּנוּ הַפָּסוּק: "וְרֵאשִׁית עֲרִיסוֹתֵיכֶם תִּתְּנוּ
> לַכֹּהֵן לְהָנִיחַ בְּרָכָה אֶל בֵּיתֶךָ".

May it be Your will, our G-d, the G-d of our Fathers, that You bless our dough, as You blessed the dough of our Mothers, Sarah, Rivkah, Rachel and Leah. And may we be blessed as in the verse: "You shall give the first yield of your dough to the kohen to make a blessing rest upon your home." (Ezekiel 44:30)

● Some have the custom to recite the following verse twice before reciting the blessing for separating challah (*Sefer Chukei HaNashim*):

> וִיהִי נֹעַם אֲדֹנָי אֱלֹהֵינוּ עָלֵינוּ וּמַעֲשֵׂה יָדֵינוּ כּוֹנְנָה עָלֵינוּ
> וּמַעֲשֵׂה יָדֵינוּ כּוֹנְנֵהוּ.

May the pleasantness of the L-rd our G-d be upon us; establish for us the work of our hands; establish the work of our hands (Psalms 90:17).

יְהִי רָצוֹן מִלְּפָנֶיךָ יְיָ אֱלֹהֵינוּ וֵאלֹהֵי אֲבוֹתֵינוּ, שֶׁהַמִּצְוָה שֶׁל
הַפְרָשַׁת חַלָּה תֵּחָשֵׁב כְּאִלּוּ קִיַּמְתִּיהָ בְּכָל פְּרָטֶיהָ וְדִקְדּוּקֶיהָ,
וְתֵחָשֵׁב הֲרָמַת הַחַלָּה שֶׁאֲנִי מְרִימָה, כְּמוֹ הַקָּרְבָּן שֶׁהֻקְרַב עַל
הַמִּזְבֵּחַ, שֶׁנִּתְקַבֵּל בְּרָצוֹן. וּכְמוֹ שֶׁלְּפָנִים הָיְתָה הַחַלָּה נְתוּנָה
לַכֹּהֵן וְהָיְתָה זוֹ לְכַפָּרַת עֲוֹנוֹת, כָּךְ תִּהְיֶה לְכַפָּרָה לַעֲוֹנוֹתַי, וְאָז
אֶהְיֶה כְּאִלּוּ נוֹלַדְתִּי מֵחָדָשׁ, נְקִיָּה מֵחֵטְא וְעָוֹן. וְאוֹכַל לְקַיֵּם
מִצְוַת שַׁבַּת קֹדֶשׁ וְהַיָּמִים הַטּוֹבִים עִם בַּעֲלִי (וִילָדֵינוּ), לִהְיוֹת
נִזּוֹנִים מִקְּדֻשַּׁת הַיָּמִים הָאֵלֶּה. וּמֵהַשְׁפָּעָתָהּ שֶׁל מִצְוַת חַלָּה, יִהְיוּ
יְלָדֵינוּ נִזּוֹנִים תָּמִיד מִיָּדָיו שֶׁל הַקָּדוֹשׁ בָּרוּךְ הוּא, בְּרֹב רַחֲמָיו
וַחֲסָדָיו, וּבְרֹב אַהֲבָה, וְשֶׁתִּתְקַבֵּל מִצְוַת חַלָּה כְּאִלּוּ נָתַתִּי מַעֲשֵׂר.
וּכְשֵׁם שֶׁהִנְנִי מְקַיֶּמֶת מִצְוַת חַלָּה בְּכָל לֵב, כָּךְ יִתְעוֹרְרוּ רַחֲמָיו שֶׁל
הַקָּדוֹשׁ בָּרוּךְ הוּא לְשָׁמְרֵנִי מִצַּעַר וּמִמַּכְאוֹבִים כָּל הַיָּמִים, אָמֵן:

May it be Your will, our G-d, the G-d of our Fathers, that the
mitzvah of separating challah be considered as if I observed
every one of its details. May my raising of the challah be
considered as the sacrifice that was offered on the altar,
which was willingly accepted. Just as giving the challah to the
kohen in the past served to atone for sins, so may it atone
for my sins and I shall be like a person reborn, free of sin
and transgression. May I be able to observe the holy Shabbat
and Festivals with my husband (and our children), and be
nourished from the holiness of these days. May the influence
of the mitzvah of challah enable our children to be always
nourished by the hands of the Holy One blessed be He, with
His abundant mercy, loving-kindness, and great love; and the
mitzvah of challah be accepted as though I have given a tithe.
And now, as I am fulfilling the mitzvah of challah with all my
heart, so may the compassion of the Holy One Blessed be He
be aroused to keep me from sorrow and pain always, Amen.

● Some have the custom to recite the following prayer after the blessing for separating challah:

יְהִי רָצוֹן מִלְפָנֶיךָ, יְיָ אֱלֹהֵינוּ וֵאלֹהֵי אֲבוֹתֵינוּ, שֶׁיִּבָּנֶה בֵּית הַמִּקְדָּשׁ בִּמְהֵרָה בְיָמֵינוּ, וְתֶן חֶלְקֵנוּ בְּתוֹרָתֶךָ.

May it be Your will, L-rd our G-d and G-d of our fathers, that the Holy Temple be speedily rebuilt in our days, and grant us our portion in Your Torah.

● A prayer for the Redemption:

יְהִי רָצוֹן מִלְפָנֶיךָ רִבּוֹנוֹ שֶׁל עוֹלָם, שֶׁתִּבָּנֶה בֵּית הַמִּקְדָּשׁ בִּמְהֵרָה בְיָמֵינוּ, שֶׁתְּרַחֵם עַל כָּל אִישׁ וְאִשָּׁה, קָטָן אוֹ גָדוֹל, יָחִיד אוֹ רַבִּים מֵעַמְּךָ יִשְׂרָאֵל, אֲשֶׁר הֵם שְׁרוּיִים בְּצַעַר. אָנָּא ה', הַצִּילֵם מִצָּרוֹתָם, בָּרְכֵם מִבִּרְכוֹתֶיךָ, הַחֲזִירֵם בִּתְשׁוּבָה שְׁלֵמָה וְתִגְאָלֵנוּ גְּאוּלָה שְׁלֵמָה לְמַעַן שְׁמֶךָ, כְּמוֹ שֶׁכָּתוּב: "וְהָיָה יְיָ לְמֶלֶךְ עַל כָּל הָאָרֶץ בַּיּוֹם הַהוּא יִהְיֶה יְיָ אֶחָד וּשְׁמוֹ אֶחָד".

May it be Your will, Master of the Universe, that You speedily build the Temple, that You will be merciful with every man and woman, minor and adult, any individual and the multitude of Your people Israel, and all who are in sorrow. O G-d, save them from their sorrow, bless them with Your blessings, cause them to return to You completely, and redeem us through a complete redemption for the sake of Your name, as it is written: "And the L-rd shall be king over all the earth, on that day the L-rd shall be one, and His name one".

● A prayer for offspring:

רִבּוֹנוֹ שֶׁל עוֹלָם, אַתָּה צִוִּיתָנוּ לְהַפְרִישׁ חַלָּה כְּדֵי שֶׁתִּשְׁרֶה
הַבְּרָכָה בָּעִסָּה כְּשָׂרָה אִמֵּנוּ עָלֶיהָ הַשָּׁלוֹם. יְהִי רָצוֹן מִלְּפָנֶיךָ
שֶׁתְּהֵא מִצְוַת חַלָּה שֶׁקִיַּמְתִּי לִזְכוּתָהּ שֶׁל _____ בַּת _____
לְפָקְדָה בְּזֶרַע שֶׁל קַיָּמָא עִם בַּעֲלָהּ וִיבֹרְכוּ בִּפְרִי בֶּטֶן וּבְכָל
מַעֲשֵׂה יְדֵיהֶם. אָמֵן.

Master of the Universe, You have commanded us to
separate challah so that our dough will be blessed as it was
with Sarah, our Mother, may peace be upon her. May it
be Your will, that the mitzvah of separating challah that
I performed in the name of ___ the daughter of ___ will
merit her to have fertile seed with her husband, and
that they will be blessed with fruit of the womb and all
works of their hand will bear fruit. Amen.

● Some have the custom to recite Psalms 25 and 34 *(Otzar Dinim
La'ishah Ve'Labat).*

37

"...The informal prayers that women are accustomed to whisper before and after candle-lighting, in which they request that G-d light up their home with domestic harmony and with children radiating reasons for joyful satisfaction; the unsophisticated requests that women customarily make before and after they fulfill the mitzvah of challah by separating part of their dough, when they ask that their family be blessed with an ample livelihood so that they will be able to support Torah scholars and contribute generously to charitable causes; the homespun prayers that women customarily utter before and after immersion in a mikveh, when they ask to be blessed with fine and healthy children who will grow up to be pious and upstanding men and women. All of these customs are Torah."

(Likutei Dibburim volume 4, page 63)

Customs and *Segulot*

The following are some special spiritual benefits credited to the mitzvah of separating challah, along with some customs practiced while performing the mitzvah of seperating challah:

● While preparing challah and other foods for Shabbat, it is customary to say, *"lichvod Shabbat kodesh,"* "in honor of the holy Shabbat."

● Some have the custom, while kneading the dough, to recite Psalms and pray for people who are in need of G-d's help and salvation.

● Because of the great merit credited to the mitzvah of separating challah, it is worthy to bake especially for the sake of fulfilling this mitzvah at least once a year, ideally during the Ten Days of Repentance *(Siddur Kol Eliyahu)*.

● The following custom has recently become common in Jewish communities: Forty women devote their prayers while separating challah to the merit of a person in need of salvation (such as recovery from illness, a worthy mate, or the birth of a child).

● The mitzvah of separating challah is recognized as a *segulah* for an easy, safe birth. It is customary to separate challah at least once in the ninth month of pregnancy.

● According to our Sages, the mitzvah of separating challah brings with it a blessing for a good livelihood into our home.

THE ART OF BAKING

Helpful Utensils

It's always good to have the right equipment on hand when you are baking. This will make your challah baking easier and more efficient – and help ensure good results.

Fine-Mesh Sifter

Flour can become wormy or bug-infested, even in a closed package, so it's important to sift the flour before you use it. The holes in a fine-mesh sifter are sufficiently small to ensure that no unwelcome guests enter the dough. Sifted flour may be kept in the freezer for a long time, and there is no need to sift it again before using it.

Bowls

It's preferable to have a variety of different-size bowls for baking. Use a small bowl for dissolving yeast, a medium-size bowl for mixing dry ingredients, and a large bowl for kneading. This bowl should be large enough to hold the dough after it has risen. Plastic bowls might not be very attractive, but they're practical and inexpensive.

Measuring Cup

A proper measuring cup will make it easy for you to measure accurate amounts of both dry ingredients and liquids, which helps ensure successful results. It will also enable you to easily calculate the amount of flour necessary to fulfill the mitzvah of separating challah.

Basting Brush

A basting brush is used for brushing raw egg on the braided unbaked loaves of dough. It also comes in handy for greasing the bread pans.

Sharp Knife

A sharp, smooth-edged knife is useful for dividing the dough before braiding challah and for scoring the dough before baking bread. It will ensure that the dough cuts cleanly and doesn't tear.

Scale

A food scale is a great help when preparing challah, especially for determining whether or not you should separate challah from the dough you're preparing.

Weights, Measures, Degrees

Approximations meant for simple practical use.

Liquid Measurements:	1 cup = 8 ounces = 230 milliliters
Dry Measurements:	1 kg = about 2 lbs.
	500 g (½ kg) = about 1 lb.
	100 g = 3.5 ounces
Length Measurements:	1 inch = 2.5 centimeters
Oven Temperatures:	Low heat = 160° C = 300° F
	Medium heat = 180° C = 350° F
	High heat = 200° C = 400° F
Flour:	1 cup white flour = about 5 ounces = 130 grams
	1 kilogram white flour = about 7 cups
	1 lb. flour = 3–4 cups
	5 lbs. flour = about 17.5 cups
Sugar:	1 cup white sugar = 7 ounces = 200 grams
Yeast:	For a recipe with 1 kilogram, or 7 cups, of flour, we use:
	2 tablespoons dry yeast = 3 pkg. dry yeast = 1 pkg. fresh yeast
	1 pkg. fresh yeast = 2 ounces = 57 grams
	1 pkg. dry yeast = ¼ ounce = 7 grams
Margarine:	1 cup margarine = 2 sticks = ½ lb. = 200 grams

Ingredients

Flour

Challah is usually made with wheat flour. You can use either white flour or whole-wheat flour.

White flour is produced by grinding the wheat kernels after the hulls have been removed. Flour should be sifted before use. Sifting eliminates the possibility of insects in the dough and also gives the flour a powder-like consistency, preventing the

formation of lumps when it is mixed with other ingredients. It is best to store sifted flour in the freezer. There is no need to resift frozen sifted flour before using it.

Whole-wheat flour is produced by grinding wheat kernels together with the hulls. The hulls contain most of the nutrients found in wheat, so whole-wheat flour has a higher nutritional value than white flour. Baked goods made with whole-wheat flour tend to be denser and heavier; they require more yeast and liquids and a longer rising time than baked goods made with white flour.

Sifting whole-wheat flour can be slightly more tedious than sifting white flour. With some types of whole-wheat flour, many grains of flour will not make it through the holes of the sifter, so you'll have to check it by hand. If you are using whole-wheat flour that was frozen immediately after it was ground, you won't need to check it at all. The flour is sold frozen, and it should be kept in the freezer until you're ready to use it.

Yeast

Yeast is a type of fungus that grows in moist, warm conditions. This is the ingredient that causes the bread to rise. When the dough is kneaded, the yeast emits gases. This makes the dough light and airy and gives it that special texture unique to baked goods made with yeast.

In order for the yeast to flourish – and cause the dough to rise – it must be provided with a "supportive atmosphere." Other ingredients in the dough interact with the yeast and activate its unique properties.

Sugar activates yeast and brings it to life. Many challah recipes call for the yeast to be dissolved in a small amount of water and sugar before it is added to the dough. Later, sugar is added along with other ingredients to achieve the desired sweetness.

Yeast likes **warm water**. Cold water impedes yeast's growth; hot water can harm it. The simplest way to achieve the desired temperature is to mix a bit of boiling water with tap water and test the result with the tip of your finger. The water should be warm and pleasant to the touch.

Salt is a necessary ingredient in a yeast dough, because it hinders yeast's growth, preventing the dough from over-rising. Salt also adds flavor and color to the final product.

Make sure that the salt doesn't touch the yeast, because direct contact with the salt can destroy the yest. In order to prevent this, it is advisable to first combine the flour and salt, or to add the salt only at the end of the kneading process.

Various Types of Yeast

Dry yeast

The main advantage of dry yeast is that it does not need to be dissolved in water before use; it can be added directly to the flour. Dry yeast has less of an aftertaste than fresh yeast and it lasts longer. We used dry yeast for the recipes in this book.

Dry yeast is available in large packages, enough for many baking sessions. After opening the package, the yeast should be stored in a closed jar in the refrigerator.

Fresh yeast

Fresh yeast should be kept in the refrigerator until you are ready to use it. Before use, the yeast should be dissolved in warm water with a little sugar.

The recipes in this book call for dry yeast. If you prefer to use fresh yeast, see page 44 to figure out the amount to be used.

Challah Baking – Step by Step

You've followed the recipe, making sure that the ingredients are mixed just so. But that's just the beginning. You still have to knead, let the dough rise, braid, and add the finishing touches. Here are some tips to help you produce perfect challah.

Kneading

Kneading dough is a vigorous activity; you will find your entire body participating in the experience. Before all of the ingredients have been joined to form one lump of dough, it's best to knead the dough in a bowl. Once you have a ball of dough, you can transfer it to a floured surface and continue kneading comfortably.

Using the heel of your hand, press on the dough and knead it away from you. Then turn the dough toward you and repeat. If you are a beginner, don't worry; just keep working with sure and steady hands. It doesn't matter exactly how you knead – what's important is that the dough get a good workout. With time, you'll get a feeling for the rhythm of kneading and find the way that works best for you.

At first the dough tends to stick to your hands and to the bowl, but as you continue kneading, the dough begins separating from the sides of the bowl, becoming smoother and springier. So don't be too quick to add more flour if the dough feels sticky; usually all it needs is a few more minutes of kneading. If you do need to add flour, do so gradually, a few tablespoons at a time, to ensure that the dough remains soft.

How long should the dough be kneaded? The longer you knead, the better the dough. Knead for about ten minutes, until you have a smooth ball of dough that is pleasant to the touch.

Want to make sure the dough has been thoroughly worked through? Take a small piece of dough and try stretching it so thin it becomes transparent without tearing it. If you can do that, your dough is ready.

> *For successful challah baking, it's always best to add the flour to the liquids. If the dough becomes tough and dry, adding liquids will do nothing to make it springier, but it's always possible to add flour to a dough that has too much liquid. It's therefore best to add the final few cups of flour gradually, kneading a bit after each addition until the desired texture is achieved.*
>
> ● *When baking bread, you can add "surprises" to the dough that will enrich the bread's taste and make it more interesting. Here are some additions you might like to try: sunflower seeds, pumpkin seeds, wheat groats, sun-dried tomatoes, onion flakes, minced garlic, nuts, and oatmeal.*

Kneading with a Mixer

You can also use a mixer to prepare challah dough. Place the ingredients in the mixer bowl and begin mixing at low speed until a dough is formed. Then increase the speed and let the mixer knead the dough for approximately seven minutes.

Most standard mixer bowls are suitable for preparing dough made with 7 cups (1 kilogram) of flour. If the recipe calls for more, you can knead in stages: Place half the amount of each ingredient in the mixer and knead. Do the same with the other half of the ingredients, and then join both doughs together.

Rising

Often we find that it is during the quiet, restful times that great things happen. When dough is left to rest, the yeast reproduces and emits gases that cause the dough to rise until it doubles, or more, in volume.

Generally, challah dough needs to rise twice before being baked:

The first rising –When you finish kneading the dough, grease the dough and your large bowl with a bit of oil to prevent the dough from drying out while rising. Cover the bowl with plastic wrap or a clean kitchen towel and let the dough rise until it doubles in volume.

Make sure to use a bowl that is at least twice the size of the unrisen dough, so that it will contain the dough once it rises. A warm environment, such as near the gas range or a radiator, speeds up the rising process.

How long does it take for dough to rise? There's no absolute answer. Dough made with white flour generally needs about an hour to rise. Dough containing whole-wheat flour is denser, so it takes longer to rise.

Once the dough has risen, filling the bowl, it is time to fulfill the mitzvah of separating challah (see "The Mitzvah of *Hafrashat Challah*").

Now the dough can be roused from its nap, the air trapped inside it removed by a brief kneading session. This second kneading ensures a soft, springy challah. Shape the loaves as desired and place them in a pan for the **second rising**.

Bear in mind that the loaves will double in volume even before they are baked and will continue to rise during the baking process. Therefore, make sure to leave sufficient space between loaves in the pan. Most oven pans can hold two large challahs or eight to ten rolls.

Braiding

After the dough has risen for the first time, it's time to shape the loaves. Use a sharp knife to divide the dough into equal-size parts to be braided. Work each piece of dough into a ball by kneading it briefly on a floured surface. Then flatten the ball and form a strand of the length you desire. Sometimes the dough is very soft; if that's the case, working with greased hands makes braiding much easier.

There are many ways to braid loaves aside from the traditional three-strand braided challah. You'll find ideas for different-shaped challahs and braiding techniques in the last section of this book, "The Art of Braiding."

For especially airy challah: After dividing the dough into parts to be braided, use a rolling pin to roll each part into a flat sheet of approximately ¼ inch (about ½ centimeter) thickness. Then roll the flat sheet jellyroll fashion and work it so that the seam disappears. Now the strands are ready for braiding.

Before braiding the loaves, prepare pans greased with oil or margarine, or lined with baking paper, so that you can place each loaf in the pan for additional rising as soon as you finish braiding it. If you leave the loaves to rise on the work surface, they're liable to flatten when you transfer them to a baking pan.

Leaving the dough at room temperature for too long can affect the quality of the challah. If you are baking a large amount of challahs, it's best to keep the dough in the refrigerator and take out as much as you need for braiding one challah at a time.

When Baking Bread

Bread can be baked in aluminum pans, clay pans, tin-cans, or any other fireproof dish. The dough can also be worked into a flat ball to make a round loaf, and be placed to bake on a baking tray lined with baking paper, or in a small round pan.

Before placing the bread in the oven, slit the loaf to allow gases to escape during baking without causing the dough to crack. Use a sharp, smooth-edged knife; a knife that is not sufficiently sharp is liable to tear the dough. You can make one long slit along the length of the loaf or a number of diagonal slits. For a rustic, country-like look, score the loaf with vertical and horizontal slits, forming a checkerboard pattern.

Glazing

Glazing adds color and beauty to the challah. The challah can be glazed immediately after the loaf is shaped, before it rises for the second time, but bear in mind that once the loaf rises, it won't be completely covered by the glaze. It's even better to glaze the loaves just before placing them in the oven, but be careful to work with a light touch so that you don't flatten the dough.

Use a small basting brush to glaze the challah and then sprinkle on the topping of your choice before the glaze dries up.

The basic ingredient of any challah glaze is *egg*. You can use a whole egg or any one of its components. The *yolk* gives challah a golden color;

the *white* gives it shine. If you are using only egg whites, you should add a bit of water.

Adding a teaspoon of *sugar* to the egg gives the challah a sweet taste and a nice dark brown color. Adding a teaspoon of *oil* enhances the shine.

Toppings

Traditionally, challah is sprinkled with either *sesame* or *poppy seeds*, but you can use any of a large variety of spices as well. *Coarse salt* and *savory herbs* go well with challah that is not sweet. Whole-wheat challah can be sprinkled with *oatmeal*, *flax seeds*, and *sunflower seeds*, or, for a rustic look, with *white flour*, *whole-wheat flour*, or *rye flour*.

Baking

How long should challah be baked? At what temperature?

It's hard to provide accurate answers to these questions. The baking time depends on the type of oven, the type of challah, and your personal taste. You can remove the challah from the oven when it is golden brown but still soft, or you can continue baking until the crust turns hard and crispy. With time, you'll discover your favorite way of making challah.

It's preferable to preheat the oven before putting the challahs in it.
Rolls are baked at high heat for approximately 20 minutes.
Medium-sized challahs are baked at medium heat for 40-50 minutes.
Especially large challahs are baked at low heat for about 1 hour.

It is advisable to check the challah while it's baking. Sometimes it is necessary to turn the pan, if one side of the challah seems to be baking faster than the other.

The challah is ready when it is golden brown both on top and on bottom, feels light when lifted, and tapping on its bottom produces a hollow sound.

When the challahs are ready, remove them from the pan and let them cool on a wire rack to prevent the bottom from turning soggy.

If you're in a rush and you want to skip the second rising step, place the braided loaves in a cold oven. Then turn on the heat to 350° F (180° C) and bake until the loaves are ready. The second rising will take place in the oven, while the loaves are baking.

● *If the loaves have turned brown on top but are not sufficiently baked, you can cover them with aluminum foil and continue baking.*

Making Life Easier

Here are some tips to help make challah baking more efficient and more enjoyable:

- Greasing the bottom and sides of the bowl with a bit of oil before putting in the ingredients will prevent the dough and flour from sticking to the bowl, and will make the cleaning up easier.

- If the dough is too sticky for you, add the oil in the recipe only after the rest of the ingredients begin to form a dough. This way, the dough will be easy to work with and not sticky.

- If you've begun kneading the dough and find that it's difficult to knead, let it rest, covered, for ten minutes before trying again. The dough will be easier to work with after this rest. This also works for dough that is difficult to braid: Place the dough in the refrigerator for ten minutes before braiding.

- To speed up the rising process in a cold place, heat the oven to the lowest temperature possible. Place a bowl of boiling water on the oven floor and put an oven rack on top of it. Then place the bowl of dough on the rack and turn off the oven.

- If your oven has two baking compartments – one for meat and one for dairy – make differently shaped loaves for each so that it will be easy to differentiate between them.

- To give baked goods you've taken out of the freezer a "straight-from-the-oven" taste, defrost them almost completely, wrap in aluminum foil, and heat in the oven for 10 to 20 minutes at low heat.

- Don't rush to discard leftover home-baked challah. It's delicious in kugels and patties, or it can be used to make croutons or breadcrumbs.

Two ways to enjoy fresh challah on Shabbat without being pressed for time or messing up the kitchen on Friday:

1. You can prepare the challah dough a few days in advance, let it rise once, separate challah, and braid the loaves. Then wrap each loaf in a plastic bag or aluminum foil and freeze. The challahs should be placed on a flat surface, and care should be taken that the loaves don't get crushed until they are properly frozen.

On Friday morning, remove the frozen loaves from the freezer, unwrap them, and let them defrost in a baking pan for approximately two hours. When the loaves are defrosted, glaze them with egg, sprinkle on the topping of your choice, and let them rise (for the second time) in a warm place. Place in the oven and bake as usual.

2. You can prepare the dough on Thursday night and leave it overnight in the refrigerator in a large bowl for the first rising. Make sure to grease both the bowl and the dough well and to cover the bowl to prevent the dough from drying out. The following morning, remove the dough from the refrigerator, knead it a bit, separate challah, and let the dough reach room temperature. Shape the loaves and place them in a pan for the second rising. Then bake as usual.

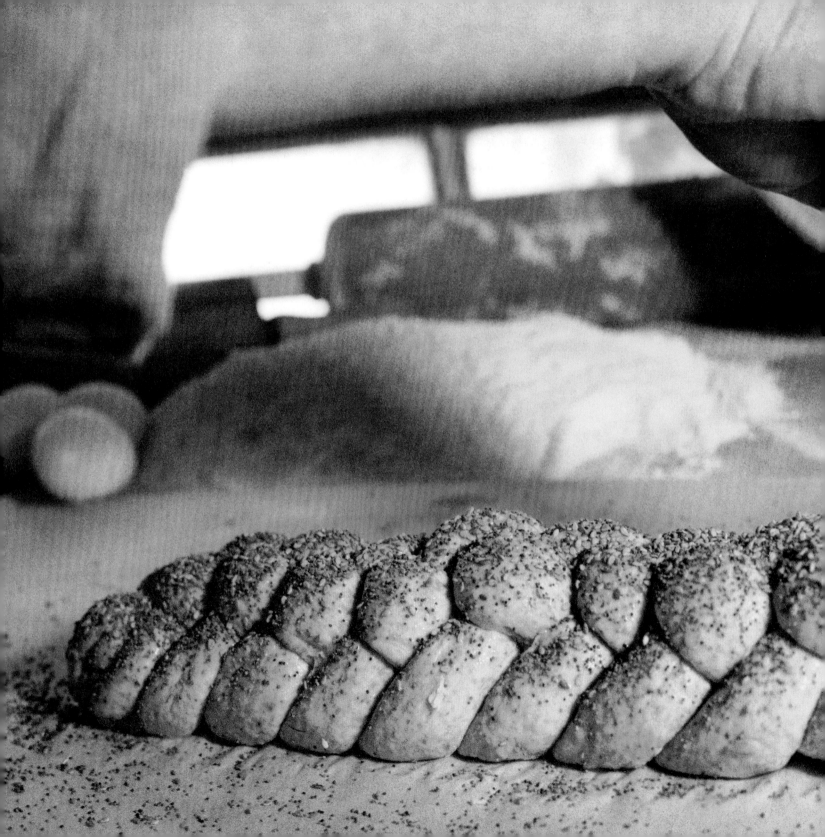

RECIPES

Heavenly Challah

The magic of simple pleasures. This challah is made with the most basic ingredients - it doesn't even contain any eggs - but anyone who tastes it admires its softness and delicious taste.

7 cups flour (1Kg)

2 tablespoons dry yeast

5–8 tablespoons sugar (depending on the desired sweetness)

2½ cups warm water

½ cup oil

1 tablespoon salt

Glaze:

1 egg, beaten

Sesame seeds

Poppy seeds

Yields:
4 medium challahs

1. Place all ingredients except the salt in a large bowl. Begin kneading. When a ball of dough is formed, add the salt.
Knead the dough for approximately 10 minutes, until the dough is smooth and soft, but not sticky.

2. Brush the dough and bowl with a bit of oil, cover the bowl with plastic wrap or a clean kitchen towel, and let the dough rise in a warm place for approximately 1 hour, until the dough doubles in volume.

3. After the dough has risen, knead it for a few minutes. Roll pieces of dough into strands to be braided. To make more airy challahs, roll out each strand into strips, approximately ¼ inch (about ½ centimeter) thick. Roll each strip jellyroll fashion to form a tube and use these to braid the challahs.

4. Place the challahs in a pan. Brush with beaten egg and sprinkle with sesame or poppy seeds. Cover and let them rise again in a warm place for approximately 40 minutes. In the meantime, preheat the oven to 350° F (180° C).

5. Bake for approximately 30 minutes, until the challahs turn golden brown. Remove the challahs from the oven and from the pan and cool on a wire rack.

Rachel's Challahs

Enjoy these soft, airy challahs.

1. In a small bowl, combine yeast, sugar, and ⅔ cup warm water. Set aside for ten minutes.

In the meantime, combine oil, eggs, water, sugar and salt in a large bowl. Mix well. Add the yeast mixture to the batter.

2. Gradually add the flour to the batter, leaving 1 cup of flour aside, and mix. At first, the batter can be mixed with a wooden spoon, but when it begins to form a dough, start kneading it with your hands. Knead the dough for about 10 minutes, until it becomes soft and pleasant, but not sticky. Add the remaining cup of flour as you knead the dough, 2 tablespoons at a time, as necessary.

3. When you finish kneading, cover the bowl with plastic wrap or a clean kitchen towel, and let the dough rise in a warm place for approximately 1 hour, until the dough doubles in volume.

4. **Separate challah**. See *"The Mitzvah of Hafrashat Challah."*

5. Knead the dough for a few minutes and then form loaves. Place the loaves in a pan, making sure to leave plenty of space between them. Brush with beaten egg and sprinkle with the topping of your choice.

Cover the loaves and let them rise again in a warm place for approximately 40 minutes, until the dough doubles in volume. In the meantime, preheat the oven to 375° F (190° C).

6. Bake for approximately 50 minutes, until the loaves turn golden brown and shiny. Remove the challahs from the oven and from the pan and cool on a wire rack.

4 tablespoons dry yeast

4 tablespoons sugar

⅔ cup warm water

1 cup oil

6 eggs

2⅔ cups warm water

4 tablespoons sugar

3 tablespoons salt

14 cups white flour
(2 Kg)

Glaze:

1 egg, beaten

Sesame seeds, zaatar, or other herb of choice

Yields:

8 medium challahs

61

Mom's Challahs

A taste of home.

4 tablespoons dry yeast

1 cup warm water

1 tablespoon sugar

3 cups boiling water

¾ cup (150 grams) margarine, softened

2 tablespoons salt

1½ cups sugar

5 eggs

14–15 cups flour

Glaze:

1 egg, beaten

Poppy seeds

Yields:

6 medium challahs

1. In a small bowl, combine yeast, 1 cup warm water, and 1 tablespoon sugar.

2. Place the margarine in a large bowl, pour the boiling water on top, and mix until the margarine is melted. Add salt and sugar and set aside for a few minutes to cool. Add eggs and mix well. Add the yeast mixture and then gradually add the flour.

3. Knead for 10 minutes. If the dough is too soft, add a bit of flour. Brush the dough with a bit of oil, cover the bowl with plastic wrap or a clean kitchen towel, and let the dough rise in a warm place for approximately 1 hour, until the dough doubles in volume.

4. **Separate challah.** See *"The Mitzvah of Hafrashat Challah."*

5. Form the loaves, place in a pan, cover, and let them rise again in a warm place for approximately 1 hour. In the meantime, preheat the oven to 350° F (180° C).

6. Brush loaves with beaten egg and sprinkle with poppy seeds. Bake for approximately 40 minutes, until the challahs turn golden brown. Remove the challahs from the oven and from the pan and cool on a wire rack.

Sweet Shabbat Challah

Especially sweet and "Shabbosdik," our families love this challah. The sweet glaze lends the challahs a special shine and festive appearance.

14 cups white flour (2 Kg)

2 tablespoons salt

4 tablespoons dry yeast

1½–2 cups sugar (to taste)

4 cups warm water

2 eggs

⅔ cup oil

Topping:

1 egg, beaten

Sesame seeds

Glaze:

¾ cup boiling water

5 tablespoons sugar

Yields: 6 challahs

1. Place the flour in a large bowl and combine with salt.

2. Add yeast, sugar, and water and then the eggs and oil. Knead the mixture well for about 5 minutes. If the dough is sticky, add a bit more flour and knead with greased hands. The dough should be smooth and very soft, but workable.

3. Cover the bowl with plastic wrap or a clean kitchen towel and let the dough rise in a warm place for approximately 1 hour, until the dough doubles in volume.

4. **Separate challah.** See *"The Mitzvah of Hafrashat Challah."*

5. Knead the dough for a few minutes on a floured surface and form the challahs. It's best to work with greased hands, since the dough is very soft.

6. Place challahs in a pan. Cover and let them rise again in a warm place for approximately 1 hour, until the dough doubles in volume. In the meantime, preheat the oven to 375° F (190° C).

7. Brush with beaten egg, and sprinkle with sesame seeds. Bake until challahs turn dark brown.

When the challahs appear to be almost done, prepare the glaze: Dissolve the sugar in boiling water. Remove the challahs from the oven and immediately spoon the boiling glaze over them. Remove the challahs from the pan so that the bottom of the challahs doesn't get wet from the glaze, and cool on a wire rack.

Chani's Shabbat Challah

"I don't like to give out my recipe," my friend Chani told me when I asked for the recipe of her tasty challahs, "because women don't like to work with sticky dough." But I finally got the recipe from her, and here it is. Highly recommended!

4 tablespoons dry yeast

5 cups warm water

⅔ cup sugar

4 eggs

2 tablespoons salt

14 cups flour (2 Kg)

½ cup oil

Glaze:

1 egg, beaten

Sesame seeds

Poppy seeds

Yields:

6 medium challahs

1. In a large bowl, combine yeast, water, and sugar. Beat eggs and add to yeast mixture. Mix the batter well.

2. In a different bowl, combine flour and salt. Add flour mixture to batter. Begin kneading. When the ingredients begin forming a dough, add the oil.

3. Knead dough for approximately 10 minutes. You may work with greased hands in order to make the kneading easier, because the dough is sticky.

Cover the bowl with plastic wrap or a clean kitchen towel and let the dough rise in a warm place for about 1 hour, until the dough doubles in volume.

4. **Separate challah.** See *"The Mitzvah of Hafrashat Challah."*

5. Transfer dough to a floured surface. Divide into parts for braiding and work each piece of dough on the floured surface until the dough is easy to work with. Braid the loaves, place in a pan, cover, and let them rise again in a warm place for approximately 40 minutes. In the meantime, preheat the oven to 350° F (180° C).

6. Brush the challahs with beaten egg and sprinkle with sesame or poppy seeds. Bake until the challahs turn golden brown. Remove the challahs from the oven and from the pan and cool on a wire rack.

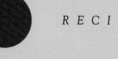

5 tablespoons dry yeast

1 tablespoon sugar

⅔ cup warm water

4 eggs

1 cup sugar

1 cup oil

⅓ cup wheat germ

2½ cups warm water

15 cups white flour

⅔ cup whole-wheat flour

1 tablespoon salt

Glaze:

1 egg, beaten

Sesame seeds

Yields:
5 large challahs

Enriched Challah

Wheat germ and whole-wheat flour enrich this challah and lend it a unique flavor.

1. In a large bowl, combine yeast, 1 tablespoon sugar, and ⅔ cup warm water. Set aside for 10 minutes. Beat eggs and add to the yeast mixture. Add sugar, oil, and wheat germ. Mix.

2. In a different bowl, combine the two types of flour and the salt. Alternately add this mixture and the water to the batter in the large bowl. Begin kneading. When the ingredients form a ball of dough, transfer to a floured surface. Knead for another 7 minutes. The dough should be soft and smooth.

3. Brush the dough and inside of the bowl with a bit of oil. Cover with plastic wrap or a clean kitchen towel and let the dough rise in a warm place for approximately 40 minutes, until the dough doubles in volume.

4. After the dough has risen, knead it for a few minutes, cover, and let it rise again in a warm place for approximately 40 minutes, until the dough doubles in volume.

5. **Separate challah.** See *"The Mitzvah of Hafrashat Challah."*

6. Form loaves and place them in a greased pan, leaving plenty of space between loaves. Cover and let them rise again in a warm place for approximately 20 minutes. In the meantime, preheat the oven to 400° F (200° C). Brush the loaves with beaten egg and sprinkle with sesame seeds.

7. Bake for 5 to 10 minutes at 400° F (200° C) and then lower the heat to 350° F (180° C). Continue baking for an additional 35 to 40 minutes, until the challahs turn golden brown. Remove the challahs from the oven and from the pan and cool on a wire rack.

Raisin Challah

Raisins add a little sweetness to this challah.

5 tablespoons dry yeast

4 cups warm water

4 eggs

½ cup oil

½ cup honey

2 cups raisins (or less, as desired)

14–15 cups flour

1 tablespoon salt

Glaze:

1 egg, beaten

Sesame seeds

Yields: 6 large challahs

1. In a large bowl, combine yeast and water. Add eggs, oil, honey, and raisins. Mix well, then add approximately half the flour and mix again.

Cover the mixture and let it rise in a warm place for about 45 minutes to 1 hour, until the mixture is bubbly.

2. Add the salt and most of the remaining flour. Mix the batter with a wooden spoon. When it forms into a dough, transfer to a floured surface and begin kneading with your hands. Gradually add the remaining flour, a little bit at a time, so that the dough will be easy to work with. The dough must remain soft.

3. **Separate challah.** See *"The Mitzvah of Hafrashat Challah."*

4. Form loaves and place in a pan. Cover loaves with plastic wrap or a clean kitchen towel and let them rise again in a warm place for about 1 hour. In the meantime, preheat the oven to 350° F (180° C).

5. Brush the challahs with beaten egg and sprinkle with sesame seeds. Bake for approximately 45 minutes to 1 hour. Remove the challahs from the oven and from the pan and cool on a wire rack.

Wonderful Sweet Challah

A rich, sweet challah similar in taste to yeast cake. A slice of this challah smeared with butter – it's Gan Eden!

1. In a large bowl, combine eggs, water, oil, and honey. Add yeast and raisins.
Add the flour gradually and then the salt. It's recommended to leave 1 cup of flour aside and add it, or a part of it, only if necessary.

2. Knead the dough for approximately 10 minutes, until you have a smooth ball that is not sticky. The dough is less airy and less springy than most yeast doughs.

3. Cover the bowl with plastic wrap or a clean kitchen towel and let the dough rise in a warm place for approximately 1½ hours. (The dough will rise, but will not double in volume).

4. After the dough has risen, knead it for a few minuets and form the loaves. Place the challahs in a pan, cover, and let them rise again for approximately 30 to 45 minutes. In the meantime, preheat the oven to 350° F (180° C).

5. Brush challahs with beaten egg and bake for approximately 40 minutes, until they turn golden brown. Remove the challahs from the oven and from the pan and cool on a wire rack.

4 eggs

1 cup warm water

1⅓ cups oil

⅔ cup honey

2 tablespoons dry yeast

¾ cup raisins

8 cups flour

2 teaspoons salt

Glaze:

1 egg, beaten

Yields: 10 small round challahs

73

Three-Color Challah

An unusual challah that will add spice and color to any meal.

1½ tablespoons dry yeast

½ cup warm water

1 teaspoon sugar

2 tablespoons oil

2 teaspoons sugar

2 eggs

7 cups flour (1 Kg)

1½ cups warm water

2 teaspoons salt

Flavorings:

6 tablespoons chopped parsley, or 4 tablespoons zaatar

4 tablespoons sweet paprika

Glaze:

1 egg yolk or 1 egg, beaten

Sesame seeds

Yields:

4 medium challahs

1. In a small bowl, combine yeast, warm water, and 1 teaspoon sugar. Mix slightly and set aside for 10 minutes.

2. In a large bowl, combine the remaining ingredients, except for the flavorings. Add the yeast mixture and knead for approximately 5 minutes, until you have a soft, springy dough.

3. Brush the dough with oil and place in a bowl. Cover the bowl with plastic wrap or a clean kitchen towel and let the dough rise in a warm place for approximately 1 hour, until the dough doubles in volume.

4. After the dough has risen, divide it into three equal parts. Work the parsley or zaatar through one part and the paprika through another, leaving the third part as it is. The result is three different-colored pieces of dough. Prepare three-strand challahs, each braided with one strand of each color.

5. Place the loaves in a greased baking pan. Brush with egg and sprinkle with sesame seeds. Cover and let them rise again in a warm place for approximately 40 minutes, until the loaves double in volume. In the meantime, preheat the oven to 400° F (200° C).

6. Bake until the challahs turn brown. Remove the challahs from the oven and from the pan and cool on a wire rack.

Half-and-Half Challah

The combination of white flour and whole-wheat flour in this challah contributes to its delicious flavor and nutritional value, yet ensures that it remains airy.

4 tablespoons dry yeast

1 cup warm water

8 cups white flour

6 cups whole-wheat flour

⅔ cup sugar

1 cup oil

2 tablespoons salt

4 eggs

3 cups warm water

Glaze:

1 egg, beaten

1 teaspoon water

Sesame seeds

Yields: 5 challahs

1. In a small bowl, combine yeast with 1 cup warm water and set aside. In a large bowl, combine the white flour and whole-wheat flour. Form a hollow in the center and pour into it the sugar, oil, salt, and eggs.

2. Add 3 cups warm water and the yeast mixture. Knead for 5 to 10 minutes until a smooth dough is formed.

3. Grease the bowl and brush the dough with oil. Cover the bowl with plastic wrap or a clean kitchen towel and let the dough rise in a warm place for approximately 1½ to 2 hours, until the dough doubles in volume.

4. **Separate challah.** See *"The Mitzvah of Hafrashat Challah."*

5. Knead the dough for a few minutes and form loaves. Place the challahs in a pan, cover, and let them rise again in a warm place for approximately 1 hour. In the meantime, preheat the oven to 350° F (180° C).

6. In a small bowl, beat the egg with 1 teaspoon water. Brush the challahs with the mixture and sprinkle with sesame seeds. Bake for approximately 45 minutes, or until the loaves turn golden brown. Remove the challahs from the oven and from the pan and cool on a wire rack.

Whole-Wheat Challah

*Easy-to-prepare challah. Proper kneading of the dough and sufficient
rising time ensure light, airy challahs.*

1. In a large bowl, combine yeast with warm water. Add oil, honey (or sugar), and eggs. Add about 6 cups whole-wheat flour and mix well. Cover the bowl with plastic wrap or a clean kitchen towel and let the dough rise in a warm place for approximately 45 minutes to 1 hour, until the dough doubles in volume.

2. Add the salt and most of the remaining flour and knead the dough for approximately 10 minutes, until a soft, smooth ball of dough is formed. If the dough is sticky, add a bit of flour – just enough to make it comfortable to work with.

3. **Separate challah.** See *"The Mitzvah of Hafrashat Challah."*

4. Form loaves, place in a pan, cover, and let them rise again in a warm place for approximately 45 minutes to 1 hour. In the meantime, preheat the oven to 350° F (180° C).

5. Brush the loaves with beaten egg and sprinkle with sesame seeds. Bake for approximately 45 minutes, until the loaves turn golden brown. Remove the challahs from the oven and from the pan and cool on a wire rack.

5 tablespoons dry yeast

5 cups warm water

⅔ cup oil

⅔ cup honey (or sugar)

5 eggs

15–16 cups whole-wheat flour

1 tablespoon salt

Glaze:

1 egg, beaten

Sesame seeds

Yields:
5–7 challahs

Rye-Oatmeal Challah

Preparing this challah takes a little more time and effort, but you'll find it's worthwhile. The result is a delicious challah that's tasty and wholesome.

6 tablespoons dry yeast

2 cups warm water

2 tablespoons honey

1½ cups honey

3 cups warm water

7 eggs

1 cup oil

3½ tablespoons salt

3 cups rye flour

4 cups oatmeal

8–9 cups whole-wheat flour

3 cups white flour

Glaze:

1 egg, beaten

Sunflower, flax, sesame, or poppy seeds

Yields: 7 medium challahs

1. In a small bowl, combine yeast, 2 cups warm water, and 2 tablespoons honey. Set aside.

In a large bowl, combine 1½ cups honey, 3 cups warm water, eggs, oil, and salt. Add the yeast mixture to the large bowl.

2. Add rye flour, oatmeal, whole-wheat flour, and white flour and begin kneading. If the mixture is sticky, add more white flour. Transfer the dough to a floured surface and knead for approximately 15 minutes.

3. Brush the dough with oil and place in a bowl. Cover the bowl with plastic wrap or a clean kitchen towel and let the dough rise in a warm place for approximately 1½ to 2 hours.

4. **Separate challah.** See *"The Mitzvah of Hafrashat Challah."*

5. Knead the dough for approximately 5 to 10 minutes and form loaves. Place loaves in a pan, cover, and let them rise again in a warm place for approximately 1 to 2 hours. In the meantime, preheat the oven to 350° F (180° C).

6. Brush challahs with beaten egg and sprinkle with seeds. Bake for approximately 45 minutes, until the loaves turn golden brown. Remove the challahs from the oven and from the pan and cool on a wire rack.

Date Challah

The date spread lends the challah a gentle sweetness and a reddish-brown color. Delicious!

7 cups whole- wheat flour

1½ tablespoons salt

2 tablespoons dry yeast

1 tablespoon sugar

1 egg

¾ cup date spread

2 cups warm water

½ cup oil

Glaze:

1 egg, beaten

Sesame or poppy seeds

Yields: 3 large challahs

1. In a large bowl, combine flour and salt. Add remaining ingredients and begin kneading. Knead for approximately 15 minutes, until a smooth ball of dough is formed.

2. Cover the bowl with plastic wrap or a clean kitchen towel and let the dough rise in a warm place for approximately 1½ hours, until the dough doubles in volume.

3. After the dough has risen, transfer it to a floured surface and form loaves. Place loaves in a pan, cover, and let them rise again in a warm place for approximately 1 hour. In the meantime, preheat the oven to 350° F (180° C).

4. Brush challahs with beaten egg and sprinkle with sesame or poppy seeds.

5. Bake for approximately 50 minutes, until the loaves turn golden brown. Remove the challahs from the oven and from the pan and cool on a wire rack.

Variation: Add 1 cup of coarsely chopped nuts to the dough.

Home-style Bread

Easy-to-prepare bread that adds a home-baked flavor to any meal.

1. In a large bowl, combine yeast, water, sugar, egg, and desired seeds. Add most of the flour, leaving about 1 cup aside. Add the margarine and salt and begin kneading.

2. Gradually add the remaining cup of flour, stopping when the dough seems comfortable to work with. Knead the dough well for approximately 10 minutes, until it is soft to the touch and not sticky.

3. Place the dough in a greased bowl, cover the bowl with plastic wrap or a clean kitchen towel, and let the dough rise in a warm place for approximately 1 hour, until the dough doubles in volume.

4. After the dough has risen, knead it for another few minuets and form the loaves. Place the loaves in a pan, cover, and let them rise again in a warm place for approximately ½ hour. In the meantime, preheat the oven to 400° F (200° C).

5. Bake for approximately 50 minutes, or until the bread turns brown and tapping the bottom produces a hollow sound. Remove the bread from the oven and from the pan and cool on a wire rack.

2 tablespoons dry yeast

3 cups warm water

⅓ cup sugar

1 egg

Sunflower seeds, pumpkin seeds, coarse wheat groats, oatmeal, or any other desired seeds

4 cups white flour

3 cups whole-wheat flour

½ cup (100 grams) butter-flavored margarine, cut into cubes

1 tablespoon salt

Yields: 2 loaves

83

Country Farm Bread

Bread with an old-fashioned flavor.

5 cups white flour

4 cups whole-wheat flour

1½ teaspoons salt

3 tablespoons dry yeast

2 teaspoons sugar

4 cups warm water

Yields: 2 loaves

1. In a large bowl, combine white flour, whole-wheat flour, and salt.

2. Add yeast, sugar, and warm water and mix until you have a dough that can easily be kneaded. If the dough is hard to work with, gradually add water until it becomes springy and flexible.

3. Knead the dough for approximately 10 minutes. Brush with oil on all sides and place in a bowl. Cover the bowl with plastic wrap or a clean kitchen towel, and let the dough rise in a warm place for approximately 1 hour, until the dough doubles in volume.

4. After the dough has risen, knead it for another few minutes and form the loaves. To give the bread more of a country look, you can sprinkle a bit of whole-wheat flour on the loaves. Score the loaves with a sharp knife.

5. Place the loaves in a pan, cover, and let them rise again in a warm place for approximately 40 minutes. In the meantime, preheat the oven to 400° F (200° C).

6. Bake for approximately 50 minutes, until the loaves turn brown and tapping on the bottom produces a hollow sound. Remove the bread from the oven and from the pan and cool on a wire rack.

Zaatar Bread

Zaatar, a popular Middle-Eastern spice mixture that is traditionally composed of marjoram, oregano, thyme, sesame, and sumac, gives this easy-to-prepare bread a unique flavor and delicate texture. Serve with olive oil and a vegetable salad. Not a crumb will remain…

2 tablespoons dry yeast

1 teaspoon sugar

3 cups warm water

7 cups flour (1 Kg)

1 teaspoon salt

½ cup zaatar

Olive oil

Yields: 2 loaves

1. In a large bowl, combine yeast, sugar, and water. Add the rest of the ingredients and knead for a few minutes. At first, the dough will be somewhat sticky, so it will be more comfortable to knead it with greased hands (use vegetable oil or olive oil), until the dough becomes soft and pleasant to the touch.

2. Brush dough and inside of bowl with olive oil. Cover the bowl with plastic wrap or a clean kitchen towel, and let the dough rise in a warm place for about 1 hour, until it doubles in volume.

3. After the dough has risen, knead it for a few more minutes and then form loaves. Grease two long baking pans and place the loaves inside. The loaves should reach half the height of the pan. Cover the pans with plastic wrap or a clean kitchen towel and let the loaves rise again in a warm place for approximately 40 minutes, until the dough doubles in volume. In the meantime, preheat the oven to 350° F (180° C).

4. Before placing the loaves in the oven, slit each loaf along its length with a sharp knife. Bake for approximately 45 minutes, or until a firm outer crust is formed and the bread turns light brown. Remove the bread from the oven and from the pan and cool on a wire rack.

Variation: Chop 2 medium onions and sauté in a bit of oil until golden brown. Add half of the amount to the dough, and sprinkle the other half on the loaves before baking.

Rosemary Bread

For a little variety, try this deliciously fragrant bread.

1. In a large bowl, combine all ingredients except the flour and salt.

2. Gradually add the flour, and then add the salt. Knead until you get a smooth ball of dough that is not sticky.
Brush the ball of dough with a bit of oil and place in a bowl. Cover the bowl with plastic wrap or a clean kitchen towel and let the dough rise in a warm place for approximately 1 hour, until the dough doubles in volume.

3. After the dough has risen, knead it for another few minuets and form the loaves. Place the loaves in pans. They should reach half the height of the pan. Cover and let them rise in a warm place for approximately ½ hour. In the meantime, preheat the oven to 350° F (180° C).

4. Slit each loaf with a very sharp knife. You can make one long slit along the length of the loaf, or a number of diagonal slits, or whatever design you fancy.

5. Bake for approximately 50 minutes. The bread is ready when a firm outer crust is formed and tapping on the bottom of the loaves produces a hollow sound. Remove the bread from the oven and from the pan and cool on a wire rack.

Variation: Instead of rosemary, add 2 tablespoons dried oregano, 4 cloves of garlic, minced, and 1 tablespoon dried coriander.

2 tablespoons dry yeast

2 tablespoons sugar

3 tablespoons olive oil

2 tablespoons
chopped rosemary

2½ cups warm water

7 cups flour (1 Kg)

1 teaspoon salt

Yields: 2 large loaves

1 tablespoon dry yeast

1¼ cups warm water

½ cup sugar

¾ cup (150 grams) margarine, cut into cubes

2 eggs

1 teaspoon lemon zest

⅔ cup raisins

½ cup dried apricots, chopped

½ cup coarsely chopped nuts

6½ cups flour

½ teaspoon salt

1 cup citrus-peel jam or any other jam

Glaze:

1 egg, beaten

1 tablespoon sugar

Yields: 2 loaves

90

Fruit Bread

This bread comes with sweet surprises! You can substitute the dried fruit in the recipe with any dried fruit of your choice.

1. In a large bowl, combine all ingredients except the flour, salt, and jam.

2. Add the flour gradually and begin kneading. When the ingredients begin to form a dough, add the salt. Knead for approximately 10 minutes, until the dough is soft and pleasant to the touch. Brush the dough with a bit of oil and place in a bowl. Cover the bowl with plastic wrap or a clean kitchen towel and let the dough rise in a warm place for approximately 1 hour, until the dough doubles in volume.

3. After the dough has risen, knead it for another few minutes and transfer to a floured surface. Divide the dough into two parts.

4. Roll out each part into a square 12 x 12 inches (30 x 30 centimeters). Smear jam onto each square and roll jellyroll style. Pinch the ends together and form into a loaf.

5. Place the loaves in a pan, cover, and let them rise again in a warm place for approximately 40 minutes. In the meantime, preheat the oven to 350° F (180° C).

6. After the loaves have risen, beat the egg with the tablespoon of sugar and brush the mixture onto the loaves.

7. Bake for approximately 30 minutes, until the bread turns brown and shiny. Remove the bread from the oven and from the pan and cool on a wire rack.

Mock Sourdough Bread

A bread with a unique, slightly tart flavor. You'll need to begin preparing this bread a day in advance.

For dough starter:

1 scant teaspoon dry yeast

½ cup warm water

1 cup white flour

For dough:

2 tablespoons yeast

1 cup warm water

1 scant teaspoon sugar

1 cup whole-wheat flour

1–2 cups white flour

1 teaspoon salt

Yields: 1 loaf

1. The day before you want to bake the bread, prepare the starter: Combine the dry yeast, water, and 1 cup flour to form a smooth, uniform batter. Cover with plastic wrap and leave it overnight at room temperature.

2. The following day, combine yeast, water, and sugar, in a large bowl. Add the starter that was prepared the day before and mix. Add salt, 1 cup whole-wheat flour, and 1 cup white flour and begin working the dough. Add another ½ cup of white flour and knead, until the dough becomes soft and springy. If the dough is still sticky, you may add more flour.

3. Brush the inside of the bowl with a bit of oil and place the dough inside. Cover the bowl with plastic wrap or a clean kitchen towel and let the dough rise in a warm place for about 1½ hours.

4. After the dough has risen, knead it for a few minutes and form a loaf. Grease a long baking pan and place the loaf inside. Cover and let it rise again in a warm place for about 1 hour. In the meantime, preheat the oven to 400° F (200° C).

5. Slit the loaf with a sharp knife. Bake for approximately 45 minutes, until a firm outer crust is formed and the bread turns light brown. Remove the bread from the oven and from the pan and cool on a wire rack.

Pita Bread

Fresh, warm pita bread is a delicious and novel alternative for serving guests. Pita baking is also a great activity to do with children.

1. In a large bowl, combine flour and salt. Add yeast, sugar, and water.

2. Knead for about 10 minutes, until a smooth, springy ball of dough is formed.

3. On a floured surface, use a sharp knife to divide the dough into equal parts, and form a smooth ball from each part.
Cover the balls of dough with a clean kitchen towel and let them rise in a warm place for 20 to 30 minutes.

4. Roll each ball into a round pita shape, approximately 6 inches (15 centimeters) in diameter, and ¼ inch (about ½ centimeter) thick. Cover and let them rise again in a warm place for 20 to 30 minutes. In the meantime, preheat the oven to 400° F (200° C).

5. Bake pitas in a pan for approximately 7 minutes. Carefully turn them over and bake for an additional 2 minutes. Remove the pitas from the oven and from the pan and cool on a wire rack.

7 cups white flour, or 4 cups white flour and 3 cups whole-wheat flour

1 teaspoon salt

2 tablespoons dry yeast

1 teaspoon sugar

2⅔ cups warm water

Yields: 15 pitas

Onion Rolls

Surprise your family with these delicious rolls for breakfast, lunch, or a light dinner.

1. In a small bowl, combine yeast, ½ cup warm water, and 1 teaspoon sugar. Stir lightly and set aside for about 10 minutes.

2. In a large bowl, combine the rest of the ingredients. Add the yeast mixture and knead for about 5 minutes, until a soft and springy dough is formed. Brush the dough with a bit of oil and cover the bowl with plastic wrap or a clean kitchen towel. Let the dough rise in a warm place for about 1 hour, until the dough doubles in volume.

3. In the meantime, prepare the filling: Melt margarine. Add the chopped onion, 1 tablespoon of water, and 1 egg and mix well.

4. After the dough has risen, divide it according to the desired number of rolls. Work each part into a ball on a lightly floured surface. Place the balls in a greased and floured pan, or on a sheet of baking paper. Leave sufficient space between the balls.

5. Flatten each ball with the palm of your hand. Press both thumbs into the center of each flattened ball to form a depression in the center. Fill the depression with the onion filling.

6. Brush the rolls with beaten egg and sprinkle with poppy seeds. Cover and let them rise again in a warm place for approximately 45 minutes, until the dough doubles in volume. In the meantime, preheat the oven to 400° F (200° C).

7. Bake for approximately 20 minutes, or until the rolls turn golden brown. Remove the rolls from the oven and from the pan and cool on a wire rack.

2 tablespoons dry yeast

½ cup warm water

1 teaspoon sugar

2 tablespoons oil

2 teaspoons sugar

2 eggs

7 cups flour (1 Kg)

1½ cups warm water

2 teaspoons salt

Filling:

2 medium onions, chopped

⅓ cup (70 grams) margarine

1 tablespoon water

1 egg

Glaze:

1 egg, beaten

Poppy seeds

Yields: about 20 small rolls

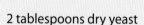

2 tablespoons dry yeast

2 cups warm water

½ cup sugar

4 eggs

7 cups flour (1 Kg)

2 teaspoons salt

1 cup oil

Filling:

Olive oil

1 medium onion, chopped

1 cup black olives, chopped, or 1 bunch basil leaves, chopped

Glaze:

1 egg, beaten

sesame seeds

Yields: 3 logs

Festive Logs

*Having guests for Chol HaMo'ed, Chanukah, or any time?
These "logs" are sure to impress!*

1. In a large bowl, combine yeast, water, and sugar. Beat the eggs, add to the bowl, and stir. Add the flour gradually, then the salt, and finally the oil.

2. Knead for about 10 minutes, until you have a very soft dough. To make kneading easier, work with greased hands. If necessary, add more flour, but only enough to make the dough workable.

3. Brush dough and inside of bowl with a bit of oil. Cover the bowl with plastic wrap or a clean kitchen towel and let the dough rise in a warm place for about 1 hour, until it doubles in volume.

4. After the dough has risen, divide it into three equal parts. On a floured surface, knead each part for a few minutes. Roll out each part into a square, about 12 x 12 inches (30 x 30 centimeters).

5. Smear each square with olive oil and sprinkle with the filling ingredients. Roll each square jellyroll style and pinch the dough well. Place the logs seam-side down in a large pan, or in long baking pans.

6. Brush the logs with beaten egg and sprinkle with sesame seeds. Cover and let them rise again for approximately 40 minutes. In the meantime, preheat the oven to 350° F (180° C).

7. Bake until the logs turn golden brown. Remove the logs from the oven and from the pan and cool on a wire rack.

Variation: Before placing the filling, spread the squares of dough with Israeli-style white cheese, instead of the olive oil.

Bagels

Bagels are easier to make than you'd think!
This recipe is worth a try.

1½ tablespoons dry yeast

1½ cups warm water

2 tablespoons sugar

2 teaspoons salt

4½ cups flour

Poppy seeds
or sesame seeds

Yields: 12 bagels

1. In a large bowl, combine yeast and ½ cup water. Add the rest of the water, sugar, flour, and salt and knead for approximately 10 minutes. If necessary, add a bit more flour until you have a soft and springy dough.

2. Brush the dough and inside of the bowl with a bit of oil. Cover the bowl with plastic wrap or a clean kitchen towel and let the dough rise in a warm place for approximately 15 minutes.

3. Work the dough on a floured surface and divide it into 12 equal parts. Work each part into a smooth ball. From each ball form a strip approximately 6 inches (15 centimeters) long. Pinch the two ends of each strip together to form a ring. Place the rings on a sheet of baking paper that was greased with a bit of oil. Cover with a clean kitchen towel and let them rise again in a warm place for approximately 20 minutes. In the meantime, preheat the oven to 350° F (180° C).

4. Fill a large pot with water and bring to a boil. Lower the flame and carefully drop 4 bagels at a time into the water. Allow them to float for 3 to 4 minutes, remove gently, and place in a pan.

5. Sprinkle poppy or sesame seeds on each bagel and bake for 35 to 40 minutes, until the bagels turn golden brown.

Kubaneh

A traditional Yemenite delicacy that rests on a hotplate overnight and is eaten warm on Shabbat morning.

1. In a large bowl, combine flour and salt. Add sugar, yeast, margarine, and water, and knead well for approximately 10 minutes, until you have a soft, smooth ball of dough.

2. Cover the bowl with plastic wrap or a clean kitchen towel and let the dough rise in a warm place for approximately 1 hour, until the dough doubles in volume.

3. After the dough has risen, knead it for another few minutes.

4. With liberally greased hands, divide the dough into 12 balls. Place the balls in the kubaneh pot so that they reach a third of its height. Cover and let them rise again in a warm place for approximately 1 hour, until the dough doubles in volume. In the meantime, heat the oven to 400° F (200° C).

5. Place the pot in the oven, uncovered, and bake for approximately ½ an hour, until the kubaneh turns golden. Remove the pot from the oven.

6. Before Shabbat, place the pot, covered, on the hotplate for the night, and serve the kubaneh warm on Shabbat morning.

7 cups flour (1 Kg)

1 tablespoon salt

¼–½ cup sugar (depending on the desired sweetness)

2 tablespoons dry yeast

1 cup (200 grams) margarine, softened

2½ cups warm water

Kubaneh pot, or any 2-quart pot that can be used in the oven, preferably with a flat cover

Yields: 1 large kubaneh

THE ART
OF
BRAIDING

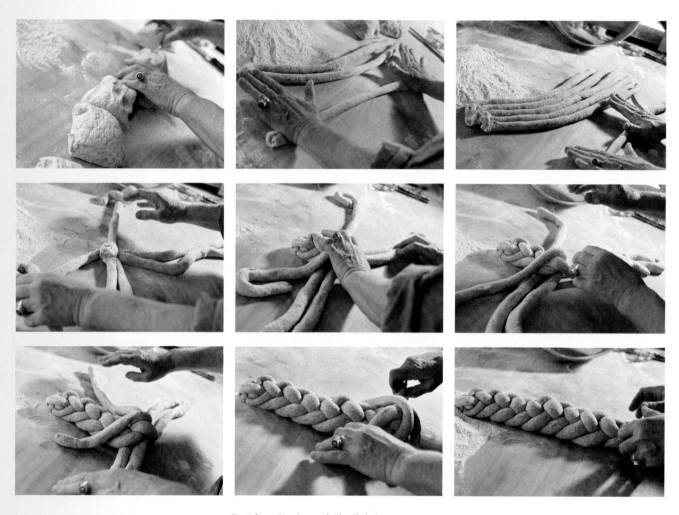

Braiding Six-Strand Challah (see page 106)

Please note, the measurements in this chapter are all approximations used in order to keep the instructions simple and clear. They are meant as recommendations for your convenience and as such are not neccesarily exact mathematical equivalents between U.S. and metric measurements.

Three-Strand Challah

 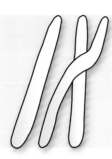 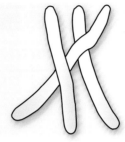

1. Divide dough into three parts. Knead each part into a smooth ball and roll each ball into a ropelike strand. Lay strands side by side.

2. Grasp the center of the right strand and cross it over the middle strand, to the center.

3. Grasp the center of the left strand and cross it over the middle strand (which previously was the right strand), to the center.

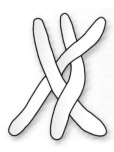  

4. Alternately repeat steps 2 and 3. When you finish braiding half the challah, pinch the ends together.

5. Turn the loaf around so that the unbraided strands face you. Move the right strand to the center **under** the middle strand. Then move the left strand to the center **under** the middle strand. When done braiding, pinch the ends together.

Four-Strand Challah

Method 1

1. Divide dough into four equal parts. Knead each part into a smooth ball and then roll each ball into a ropelike strand. Lay the strands side by side and pinch together at the top.

2. Begin braiding, similar to weaving a basket. Begin from the left and work toward the right: grasp the leftmost strand (number 1) and weave it over the next strand (number 2), under the next strand (number 3), and over the rightmost strand (number 4).

3. Repeat with the strand that is now the leftmost strand (number 2): weave it over the next strand (number 3), under the next strand (number 4), and over the rightmost strand (number 1).

4. Continue working from left to right.

5. Pinch the ends together and tuck them under the loaf for a nice finish.

Four-Strand Challah

Method 2

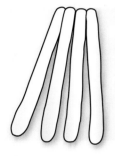 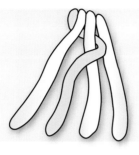 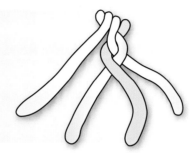

1. Divide dough into 4 equal parts. Knead each part into a smooth ball and roll each ball into a ropelike strand. Lay the strands side by side and pinch together at the top.

2. Grasp the leftmost strand and pass it to the right, under the two strands adjacent to it, and then back toward the left, over one strand (the one closest to it now).

3. Grasp the rightmost strand and pass it to the left, under the two strands adjacent to it (which have already been braided), and then back to the right, over one strand.

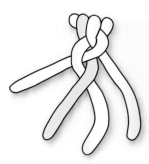 

4. Alternately repeat steps 2 and 3.

5. When done braiding, pinch the ends of the strands together.

Six-Strand Challah

See photographs on page 102

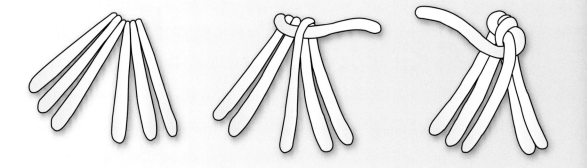

1. Divide dough into six equal parts. Knead each part into a smooth ball and then roll each ball into a long (at least 10 inches, 25 centimeters) ropelike strand.
Lay the strands side by side in two groups of three and pinch the ends of the strands together at the top.

2. Take the leftmost strand in your left hand and the rightmost strand in your right hand. Weave the left strand under the right strand and place it at the upper right corner.
Weave the right strand over the left strand toward the center, so that there are two strands on either side of it.

3. Take the rightmost strand (the one that was moved to the right in step 2) in your right hand, and the one on its immediate left in your left hand. Moving both hands simultaneously to the left, place the strand in your left hand at the upper left corner, and place the strand in your right hand at the center.

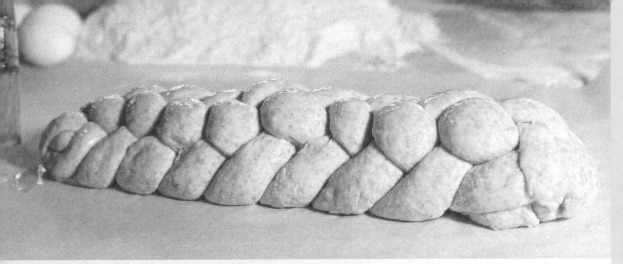

4. Take the leftmost strand (the one that was moved to the left in step 3) in your left hand, and the one on its immediate right in your right hand. Moving both hands simultaneously to the right, place the strand in your right hand at the upper right corner, and place the strand in your left hand at the center.

5. Alternately repeat steps 3 and 4.

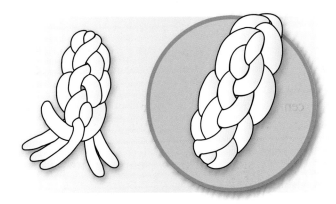

6. When done braiding, pinch the ends of the strands together.

One-Strand Challah

 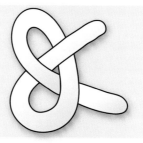 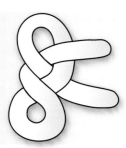

1. Form a ball of dough into a ropelike strand 25–30 inches (about 60–80 cm) long. On your work surface, arrange the strand as shown.

2. Thread the left end of the strand through the loop so that you have a knot shape.

3. Grasp the lower loop and twist it to the right, so that a smaller loop is formed.

4. Thread the lower end of the strand through the lower loop, from the top of the loaf.

5. Grasp the upper loop and twist it to the left, so that a smaller loop is formed.

6. Thread the upper end through the upper loop, from the underside to the top of the loaf.

Rose Challah

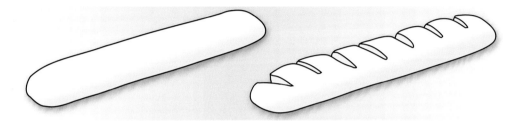

1. Form a ball of dough into a ropelike strand 12 inches (30 cm) long and 1 inch (about 2 cm) thick. Flatten the strand into a flat log, 2 inches (about 4 cm) wide.

2. Cut diagonal slits reaching halfway across the log at about 1.5 inches (about 4 cm) intervals.

3. Coil the log around itself and pinch the end.

4. Stand up the rose challah in a pan.

Festive Knot Rolls

1. Form a ball of dough and roll it into a long, ropelike strand, about 12 inches (30 cm) long and 1 inch (about 2 cm) in diameter.

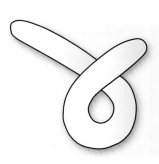  

2. Form a loop with one long end and one short end, as shown.

3. Thread the long end through the loop.

4. Pinch the two ends together on the bottom of the roll.

Figure-Eight Rolls

1. Form a ball of dough and roll it into a long, ropelike strand, about 12 inches (30 cm) long and 1 inch (about 2 cm) in diameter.

2. Arrange the strand as shown.

3. Grasp the short end in your left hand, and with your right hand pass the long end under the short end. Thread the long end through the loop, from the top of the roll to the bottom.

111

Specialty Shapes

Family Challah

Prepare as many balls of dough as there are members in your family and arrange them tightly in a pan (a round pan works best).

Blossom Challah

Form different-shaped rolls and, as with the family challah, arrange them in a symmetrical pattern in a round pan.

The result: a large, unique challah perfect for festive occasions.

Crown-Shaped Challah

- Roll a small ropelike strand in a jellyroll fashion.

- Encircle it with a ring made of two strands coiled around each other.

- Finally, add a strand to form a ring around the first two.

Double-Decker Challah

● Form six ropelike strands of equal length – three thick ones and three thin.

● Braid the three thick strands together and then braid the three thin strands together.

● Place the thin braid on top of the thick braid and tuck the ends under the thick braid.

Twists

Form two ropelike strands and coil them around each other.
Join the ends to form a ring.

Ring Challah

● Braid a three-strand challah from three very long strands and arrange it in a ring shape in a round pan.

● Place a round can in the center so that when the dough rises, the challah's shape will be preserved.

● Remove the can before baking.

Five-Ringed Challah

Divide dough into five equal parts. Knead each part into a smooth ball and then roll each ball into a ropelike strand.
Form each strand into a ring, connecting it to the next ring as in a chain.

Tin-Can Bread

For a unique home-baked gift, why not bake a loaf of bread in a tin-can?
Thoroughly grease a clean tin-can. Place inside it a ball of dough that takes up approximately half the can and let it rise.
Bake until the top turns golden brown and crusty.
Carefully remove the bread from the can and cool on a wire rack.

Star-of-David Challah

Grape-Shaped Challah

"Chamsah" Challah

Challahs for
Shabbat and Festivals

For Shabbat

● Some families have the custom to place twelve small challahs on the table, in commemoration of the showbread *(lechem hapanim)* that was kept on the Table in the Temple.

● According to the custom of the Ari, twelve challahs in the form of a double *segol* were placed on the table at every Shabbat meal (two *segols* are formed using six challahs, and the other six are placed directly on top of the first six). Thus, in *"Azamer Bishevachin,"* a *piyyut* traditionally sung during the Friday night meal, the Ari writes: *"Shechinta titattar beshit nahamei listar* – May the Shechinah be adorned by the six loaves on each side." Some prepare two six-strand loaves, thus fulfilling the custom of "six on each side."

● Challahs can be baked in the shape of various symbols relevant to the weekly *parashah* (Torah portion of the week).

For Rosh Hashanah

● It has become the widespread custom in many communities to bake round challahs in honor of Rosh Hashanah. The round shape symbolizes the yearly cycle and the "wheel of time," the ascents and descents that a person experiences during his life. It also symbolizes perfection and infinity, expressing our hope for a perfect year, free of troubles and tribulations, a year of unlimited blessings.

● The traditionaly round challah of Rosh Hashanah is sometimes adorned with a "crown" made of a small braided ring of dough, commemorating the prayers of Rosh Hashanah proclaiming G-d King over the universe.

● Eastern European Jews used to bake challah in the shape of a ladder to symbolize that on Rosh Hashanah G-d decides "Who will be humbled and who will be elevated," as is stated in the prayers of Rosh Hashanah.

● In some European communities, the custom was to bake round challah reminiscent of a bird peeking out of a nest (known as *"foigel challah,"* bird challah, in Yiddish). The reason for the custom: Just as G-d shows mercy to birds, so should He have mercy on us.

● Lithuanian Jews had the custom to bake challah shaped like outstretched palms of the hand. The shape was meant to symbolize the hands of the kohens raised to bless the people during the Priestly Blessing *(Birkat Kohanim)*.

● The Jews of North Africa used to bake challah in the shape of a fish or a *"chamsah,"* a five-fingered hand, symbolizing good luck.

Before Yom Kippur

● In the Ukraine, challahs baked in honor of the special meal before the Yom Kippur fast *(seudah hamafseket)* were adorned with birds to commemorate the verse, "Like flying birds, so shall the L-rd of Hosts protect Jerusalem" (Isaiah 31:5).

For Hoshana Rabbah

● In Poland, round, coiled challah with a ladder on top was prepared in honor of Hoshana Rabbah.

● An ancient custom is to bake challah in the shape of palms of the hand, outstretched to the heavens to receive the notes upon which G-d's verdict for the upcoming year is written (Hoshana Rabbah is the last day of the High Holidays, and by tradition it is the day when the verdict for the upcoming year is sealed).

For Chanukah

● Some people have the custom to bake a challah in the shape of a Chanukah menorah (eight-branched candelabra).

For Purim

● Eastern European Jews used to prepare a challah with a flower-shaped piece of dough on it to symbolize *"Shoshanat Yaakov,"* the *piyyut* sung after the reading of Megilat Esther.

● Moroccan Jews bake a special type of bread in honor of Purim, called *"Einei Haman"* or "Haman's eyes." The custom is to distribute this delicacy for *mishlo'ach manot* as well. The bread is adorned with almonds and unpeeled hardboiled eggs. The eggs are sunken into the dough and held down by two strips of dough in an *X* shape.

The Shabbat After Pesach

● There is a custom to bake key-shaped challah in honor of the Shabbat after Pesach. This was the time of year when the Jews entered the Holy Land and the manna stopped falling from heaven. Then they began to eat from the produce of the land and to earn their livelihood in a natural manner. The key-shaped challah symbolizes the key to livelihood which is in G-d's hand, and our prayers to Him to open the gates of livelihood for us.

Another reason, based on Kabbalistic teachings, is that at midnight, on Seder night, various spiritual influences depart from the world. By working to achieve an enhanced spiritual level during the *sefirat ha'omer* period, we gradually bring them back. The key-shaped challah symbolizes the effort made on our part, as it is written, "Make for me an opening like the eye of a needle and I will open for you an opening as broad as a spacious hall." We create an opening by observing Shabbat, and we hope G-d will open for us His bountiful treasure house, as it is written, "He had commanded the skies above, and opened the doors of heaven" (Psalms 78:23).

For Shavuot

● In some European communities it was customary to prepare bread in the shape of Mount Sinai, or the tablets of the Ten Commandments.

● Some have the custom to bake a challah adorned with a ladder comprised of seven rungs, alluding to the seven heavens G-d rent apart at the time of *matan Torah* (the giving of the Torah). The numerical equivalent of the Hebrew word *sulam* (ladder) equals *Sinai*.

● An ancient custom is to bake a long loaf of bread with four heads to commemorate the two bread *(shetei halechem)* sacrifice offered on Shavuot. Why a long loaf? Because the Torah is referred to as "bread" and it is written that Torah is "longer than the earth's measure" (Job 11:9). Why four heads? To allude to the verse, "A river flowed out of Eden to water the garden, and from there it separated and became the source of four river-heads" (Genesis 2:10). Torah is compared to a river and Sinai to Eden. Another reason is that the four heads correspond to the four parts of the Torah: *peshat, remez, derash,* and *sod* (literal, allusive, hermeneutic, and secret).

Thanks

To our dear Mom and Dad, Noa and Aharon Berenson,
for the concern, wholehearted devotion and endless efforts,
in bringing this book out to the world.

To Yael, for the faithful devoted help,

To Anat, who was always there to save us,

To Avraham and Uri, for being what you are,

To beloved Josepha, thousands of thanks for the dedicated pedantic work all through the way,

To Yehudah, for pushing forward towards the goal and for the trust and partnership,

To Chanoch, for the great help that always comes from the heart; and with a smile,

To Imma Naomi, for your big assistance which came exactly on time, and for your serious and
dedicated work, that was done in the best of ways,

To our dear Tamar, and Shilo *"ha-Ezer kenegdah"*, for the gorgeous photos, the great investment
of effort and the *"neshamah yeterah"*,

To the Lubavitch Women, publishers of the book "Spice and Spirit", for the generosity and
willingness to be of aid, and for the inspiration we got from your wonderful book!

To Mrs. Chani Goldwasser for the beautiful translation,

To Mrs. Suri Brand for the expert editing – many thanks,

To Mr. Barukh Goldberg, for the accurate and thorough work of editing,

To David Hillel, for the help in editing the chapter "The Blessing in the Dough",

To Rabbi Shmuel Eliyahu, for the advice, the support and the assistance,

To Rabbi Meir Zilbershlag, for helping from the beginning till the end,

To the wonderful people of Keter Press, for the professional work and concern,

And to all the dear friends who baked, tasted, read and helped.

Illustrations on pages 103, 104, 106, 107 are by the courtesy of the Lubavitch Women's Cookbook Publications.
The Hebrew version of the prayer on page 35 is by the courtesy of Simchonim Publishers.